FIGHTING SHIPS
OF WORLD WAR II

The American and British
concepts of the 35,000-ton
battleship: U.S.S. *Washington*
(foreground) and H.M.S.
Duke of York in northern
waters in 1942

FIGHTING SHIPS
OF WORLD WAR II

J. N. WESTWOOD

SIDGWICK & JACKSON

LONDON

Acknowledgements

Foto Ferdinand Urbahns, 135
Imperial War Museum, 2, 6–7, 9, 10–11, 13, 14, 15, 18,
21 (left), 23 (top), 25, 31 (inset), 35 (inset), 39, 41, 48–9,
54 (btm), 56–7, 59, 60, 63, 65 (top), 68, 74–5, 77, 81, 82–3,
85, 89, 93, 99, 103, 105, 106–7, 108, 109, 110–11, 113 (btm),
115, 117, 122–3, 124, 127, 128, 132, 134, 138–9, 140–1, 143,
144, 145, 154, 158
J. N. Westwood, 23 (btm), 44
Robert Hunt Library, 2, 4–5, 17, 20, 21 (right), 22–3, 26–7,
29, 30–31, 33, 35, 36–7, 42–3, 46–7, 51, 52–3, 54 (top),
65 (btm), 67, 70, 73, 78–9, 80, 86, 87, 91, 95, 96–7, 101, 104,
113 (top), 119, 121, 131, 135, 136–7, 148–9, 150
Shaw Savill Line, 146–7

ISBN 0 283 98287 X

Designed by Graham Mitchener

Printed in Great Britain by
The Whitefriars Press Ltd.
London and Tonbridge
for Sidgwick and Jackson Limited
1 Tavistock Chambers, Bloomsbury Way
London WC1A 2SG

Another Japanese warship
falls victim to U.S. bombs
towards the end of the war. As
the escort vessel heels over,
its crew divides into
swimmers and non-swimmers

CONTENTS

THE BATTLESHIP 6
The Yamato 24
The Admiral Graf Spee 28
The Scharnhorst 33
The Bismarck 36
H.M.S. Duke of York 40
U.S.S. Alabama 42
U.S.S. Washington 45
H.M.S. Warspite 48
U.S.S. Texas 50
The Kongo 52

**THE AIRCRAFT
CARRIER** 56
H.M.S. Ark Royal 66
U.S.S. Enterprise 69
U.S.S. Hornet 74
U.S.S. Lexington 76
The Akagi 78
The Zuikaku 80

THE CRUISER 82
U.S.S. Indianapolis 96
The Mogami 98
U.S.S. Boise 100
H.M.S. Ajax 102
H.M.S. Belfast 105
The Prinz Eugen 108

THE DESTROYER 110
U.S.S. Johnston 118
H.M.S. Saumarez 120

THE SUBMARINE 122
The U-47 134
U.S.S. Cavalla 136
H.M.S. Thunderbolt 138

THE ESCORT 140
H.M.S. Jervis Bay 146
U.S.S. England 148

Chronology of the War at Sea 150

Index of Ships and Battles 159

THE BATTLESHIP

What use are Britain's battleships to us if they can't move on wheels?' asked a much-quoted Russian man-in-the-street in August 1914. It was a good question, because it was not Britain's proud and costly Dreadnoughts which would decide the issue of the First World War. After that war, others besides Russian men-in-the-street were questioning the role of the battleship.

Few denied the importance of sea power, but not everyone accepted the importance of the battleship. Both strategically and tactically, the ostensible role of the battleship was to be the final arbiter of any naval war. It was a ship which was more powerfully armed and armoured than any other type, and naval theory maintained that a setpiece battle between lines of battleships would determine the result of any naval war. The coming of the torpedo, which could blast holes below the waterline armour of any battleship, had earlier suggested that the latter could no longer be considered invulnerable to smaller ships, could no longer be considered the 'great deterrent' of naval warfare. But in the First World War the torpedo, despite some spectacular successes, had not really proved itself as a battleship killer. Yet no sooner had the battleship demonstrated that it could cope with the seaborne torpedo than it was confronted with another new weapon, the aeroplane. The First World War showed that the airborne torpedo and the airborne bomb were viable weapons whose development might well mean the end not only of the battleship but perhaps of all warships other than the submarine and aircraft carrier.

But the battleship's surrender to air power took much longer than the air enthusiasts anticipated. During the Second World War the aircraft carrier did finally emerge as the prime naval unit, but the battleship retained an important supporting role, especially in waters where weather made flying unreliable and where the enemy possessed heavy surface ships.

Despite the need to add aerial defence to torpedo defence the battleship remained basically the same as it had emerged from the nineteenth century. It was an armoured gun platform, intended to withstand the most heavy guns brought against it, and to be able to penetrate the armour of the strongest ship opposing it. These characteristics had meant that, with each new battleship being designed to outdo its predecessors, the size of ships had progressively increased to accommodate heavier guns, thicker armour, and the bigger engines needed to propel the greater bulk. This was one aspect of the naval race which in the decade before 1914 had influenced not only the strategy, but also the economies, of Britain and Germany.

When the First World War ended it seemed that yet another naval race would follow, which might well ruin the weakened economies of the powers and, by intensifying national rivalries, lead to another conflict. With the U.S.A. declaring its intention of building a 'navy second to none', with Japan initiating an immense new construction programme, and Britain unwilling that these two

nations should displace it as prime naval power, an impoverishing
race seemed unavoidable except through international cooperation. This cooperation, to the surprise of many, was indeed forth-
coming, and the outcome was the Washington Naval Treaty, 1922.
The treaty was welcomed by the world at large, but not by battleship designers.

So far as capital ships were concerned, the main provisions of this
rather remarkable international agreement were that by 1934
Britain was to reduce its capital ships to twenty units, the U.S.A. to
eighteen, Japan to ten, France to seven modern and three old, and
Italy to six modern and four old. This meant that most ships being
built at the time of the treaty were abandoned. Moreover, although
Britain was allowed to start two new battleships at once and France
and Italy one each in the late twenties, until 1931 no other new
battleships (or the faster and less armoured battlecruisers) were to
be started. Also, no ship was to exceed 35,000 tons, carry guns
larger than 16-inch, or be replaced by a new ship before it had
reached twenty years of age.

These provisions created new problems for designers. The
35,000-ton limitation meant that some existing designs could
no longer be accepted, even after 1931. The first of the battleships
built under the new conditions, the British *Nelson* and *Rodney*,
were strange-looking ships, being hastily redesigned from existing
plans for 47,000-ton battlecruisers. To overcome weight limitations while preserving the heavy armament of nine 16-inch guns,
their designers accepted a comparatively low speed of twenty-
three knots and at the same time placed the entire main armament
forward, with the engines and superstructure near the stern.

This arrangement was later adopted by the French; it had the advantage of concentrating the magazine spaces, thus reducing the extent of the armour.

The *Nelson* and the *Rodney* could be regarded as intermediate between the old First World War battleships and the future generation of more heavily armed and faster ships. In general, each of the naval powers adopted its own methods of coping with (or evading) the provisions of the Naval Treaty. In the interwar years Britain, Japan, Italy and the U.S.A. carried out extensive reconstructions of their older battleships, thus creating 'like-new' ships in place of the entirely new ships banned by treaty. Such reconstructions, in the extreme cases, replaced all but the hull and main guns. Thus Britain rebuilt the battleships *Warspite*, *Valiant* and *Queen Elizabeth* as well as the battlecruiser *Renown*. Thicker deck armour against bombs and plunging shells, better bulges below the waterline to absorb torpedo detonations, greater elevation of main guns to increase the range, enclosure in tower structures of the former bridges and platforms clustered around the foremast, and better anti-aircraft armaments were the usual ingredients of these changes. Because of great improvements in engine and boiler design, resulting in less weight and space being required for the same horsepower, such reconstructions could be carried out without increasing the size of the ships or reducing the speed. Fewer boilers sometimes meant that one funnel could replace two, which improved the field of fire of the anti-aircraft guns. American rebuildings were somewhat less extensive than the British: the old engines were retained, although surviving coal-burners were converted to oil-burning. At the same time the

majority of U.S. battleships lost their characteristic 'cage' masts, these being replaced by tripod structures similar to those favoured by the British navy prior to 1920. The Italians and Japanese, in their rebuildings, did raise speeds somewhat, the Italians at the expense of protection and the Japanese by means of an increase in size. Most navies equipped their battleships, rebuilt or unrebuilt, with catapults and cranes for handling one or more seaplanes: the latter were expected to be of great value for scouting and for directing gunfire.

Of other 1914 naval powers, Austria-Hungary had disappeared, and Russia could no longer be considered a naval power, even though in the late thirties she would try to obtain foreign help to build new battleships. Germany was a special case. She was forbidden by the Versailles Treaty to build any armoured ships above 10,000 tons which meant, in the minds of those who drew up that treaty, that any battleships she built would be of the same size and power as those of about 1895. However, from 1934, at first covertly and later under the provisions of the Anglo-German Naval Treaty of 1935, Nazi Germany began to build battleships.

In 1930 a further naval agreement was signed in London, but only by Britain, the U.S.A. and Japan. This allowed the U.S.A. for the first time a slight pre-eminence in battleships. Both Britain and the U.S.A. were to scrap a few ships to bring the strength of each down to fifteen units, but the U.S.A. was allowed to have a slightly higher tonnage. Japan agreed to limit her battleships to nine units. France felt unable to sign because she knew that Germany had just started to build what were later to be known as 'pocket battleships'. Since Germany was France's most likely future enemy France wished to reserve her freedom of policy. And since Italy regarded France as *her* most likely enemy, she too decided not to sign unless France did so. Then, in 1936, came the London Naval Treaty. This time Italy refused to sign because of the international pressure brought against her after her invasion of Abyssinia. Japan, too, withdrew and embarked on a well-concealed rearmament programme. Thus only the U.S.A., Britain and France were signatories. The ban on new battleships was ended, but maximum permitted size was kept at 35,000 tons. However, since the non-signatory and increasingly threatening Japan seemed likely to build much bigger ships than this, the three signatories reserved the right to abandon the 35,000-ton limit; this they did in 1938, raising the size to 45,000 tons. Meanwhile in the Anglo-German Naval Treaty of 1935 Britain, with scant reference to France or the U.S.A., agreed that Germany could rebuild her fleet, provided that she did not exceed one-third of the British strength. By that year the Nazis were well in power, and would probably have begun naval rearmament in any case, so the British could argue that their diplomacy had at least kept the inevitable within limits. Germany simultaneously agreed to conform with the size limits of the London Naval Treaty.

Thus in the late thirties, after a break of more than a decade, the

The French battleship *Richelieu* had an unusual war record; while yet uncompleted she was removed to Dakar in order to evade the invading Germans in 1940 where she fought against the British, but towards the end of the war she joined the British fleet. Here she is in the later phase of her career

powers began to build a new generation of battleships. Despite the limitations still observed by most competitors, which meant that the new ships were smaller than the ships designed but never built after the First World War, improved technology enabled higher speeds to be reached without sacrificing arms or armour. Thus the new generation was of almost a new type, the fast battleship, capable of from twenty-seven to thirty-two knots; in other words the battleship was now as fast as the battlecruiser and the latter type, never very popular because of its weak armour, was finally eclipsed.

Most of the powers had been working on designs for new ships well before the ban on new construction ended. Britain, and to a lesser extent the U.S.A., favoured an agreed limitation on the size of the new battleships, and especially a reduction of the main guns to 14-inch. Although in fact international agreement had not been reached on these limitations Britain, in order not to discourage such an agreement, did design its *King George V* series of battleships with 14-inch guns. This resulted in a class somewhat weaker than its contemporaries in other navies.

Because she had not signed the London naval agreement in 1930, Italy was enabled to become the first power to order battleships of the new generation. These were the *Vittorio Veneto* class, not all of which were completed. They were handsome ships, fast, and well armed with nine 15-inch guns. However, their role in the Second World War was small. Next to build new battleships were the Germans, who ordered the famous *Scharnhorst* and *Gneisenau* in 1934. Because they were designed and started before the Anglo-German Naval Treaty, their design was influenced by political circumstances, which is one reason why their main guns were only of 11-inch calibre. Then France, in order to match the new Italian ships, laid down the three *Richelieu* class ships, with eight 15-inch weapons. Meanwhile Germany, in a stronger position following the agreement with Britain, ordered two ships of the *Bismarck* type, also with eight 15-inch guns. Britain and the U.S.A., still striving

13

The French battleship *Dunkerque* was built to match the German pocket battleships. She is shown here at King George VI's coronation naval review in 1937

to limit the size of battleships, then laid down respectively five *King George V* units (ten 14-inch guns) and the two *Washingtons* (nine 16-inch). The latter were soon followed by four more of an improved design, the *South Dakota* type. Subsequently the U.S.A. built the 46,000-ton *Iowa* class with the same armament but much faster speed, while Britain, also after the mutual relaxation of the self-imposed 35,000-ton limitation, began the *Lion* class, with nine 16-inch guns. These were never finished owing to lack of shipyard capacity during the war.

Japan, meanwhile, had withdrawn behind a curtain of secrecy and hostility. Little information, but many rumours, leaked out about her naval programme. Such rumours sometimes had a considerable influence, as when the U.S.A. built the *Alaska* class battlecruisers to counter Japanese battlecruisers which in fact never existed. What the Japanese were really doing was not known, and would have caused considerable repercussions if it had been: they were building four monster battleships of 65,000 tons with 18-inch guns. Two of these *Yamato* type were completed in time to participate in the war, but were sunk by naval aircraft before their awesome main armaments could get into action against U.S. battleships.

The fate of the *Yamato* and her sister, sent to the bottom by literally hundreds of aircraft and never engaging with hostile battleships, exemplifies the rarity during the war of those ship against ship combats visualized by naval theorists. The history of naval design and construction was long dominated by the if-they-have-it-we-must-have-it-too concept. Navy ministries measured their construction programmes not so much by their real requirements as by the imagined need to 'match' what the potential enemy had. To a certain extent this was valid, but only to a certain extent. Firstly, it was not always possible to forecast who the next enemy would be. Secondly, simple ship against ship encounters, in which the strongest ship could be expected to win, rarely occurred. The Royal Navy did not confront the *Bismarck* or the *Scharnhorst* or the *Graf Spee* with a single ship of the same size; it was able to meet these raiders with several ships. Similarly, U.S. and Japanese battleships never encountered each other on even terms. Also, the argument that battleships were necessary as an antidote to the battleships of potential enemies was hardly confirmed in practice: the following table, showing battleship losses during the war, also indicates how few owed their demise to encounters with ships of the same type.

SECOND WORLD WAR BATTLESHIP LOSSES
(SHOWING PRIME CAUSES)

Britain

Royal Oak	U-boat; two torpedoes
Hood	Battleship; shellfire
Barham	U-boat; three torpedoes
Repulse	Japanese aircraft; five torpedoes, one bomb
Prince of Wales	Japanese aircraft; six torpedoes, one bomb

France

Bretagne	British battleships; shellfire
Strasbourg	Scuttled

U.S.A.

Oklahoma	Japanese aircraft; four torpedoes
Arizona	Japanese aircraft; one torpedo, eight bombs

U.S.S.R.

Marat	Aircraft; one or more bombs

Germany

Graf Spee	Cruisers; gunfire
Bismarck	Battleships, destroyers, aircraft; gunfire and torpedoes
Scharnhorst	Battleship, cruisers, destroyers; gunfire and torpedoes
Tirpitz	Aircraft; five bombs
Schleswig-Holstein	Scuttled after bombing
Gneisenau	Scuttled after mining and bombing
Schliesen	Scuttled after mining and bombing
Lützow	Scuttled after bombing
Scheer	Aircraft; five bombs

Italy

Conti di Cavour	British aircraft; torpedoes
Roma	German aircraft; glider bomb

Japan

Hiei	Cruisers, destroyers, aircraft; gunfire and torpedoes
Kirishima	Battleships; gunfire
Mutsu	Accidental explosion
Haruna	Bombed while laid-up
Musashi	Aircraft; twenty torpedoes, thirty-three bombs
Fuso	Battleships; gunfire
Yamashiro	Destroyers; torpedoes
Kongo	Submarine; one torpedo
Yamato	Aircraft; ten torpedoes, twenty-three bombs
Hyuga	Bombed while laid-up
Ise	Bombed while laid-up

The *Dunkerque*'s sister-ship *Strasbourg* was another French ship with a varied war record. In 1940 she was in action against the British. Then in 1942 her crew scuttled her at Toulon. In the final stages of the war she was resurrected by the Germans as a gun platform to oppose the Allied landings in southern France. Here she is shown after pounding by Allied bombers in 1944. Beside her lie the remains of a modern French light cruiser

Name	Completion year (rebuilding completion in brackets)	Tonnage	GUNS Main	Secondary	Heavy A.A.	Speed in knots	Armour (maximum thickness of side belt in inches)
U.S.S.R							
Old battleships							
Oktyabrskaya Revolyutsia	1914	23,000	12 12-in	12 4·7-in		23	9
Parizhskaya Kommuna	1914	23,000	12 12-in	16 4·7-in		23	9
Marat	1914	23,000	12 12-in	16 4·7-in		23	9

N.B. At various times in their careers these ships were named respectively *Gangut*, *Sevastopol*, and *Petropavlovsk*.

Name	Completion year	Tonnage	Main	Secondary	Heavy A.A.	Speed	Armour
U.S.A.							
Old battleships							
Arkansas	1912(1926)	26,000	12 12-in	16 5-in	8 3-in	21	11
New York	1914(1927)	27,000	10 14-in	16 5-in	8 3-in	21	12
Texas	1914(1927)	27,000	10 14-in	16 5-in	8 3-in	21	12
Nevada	1916(1929/43)	29,000	10 14-in	12 5-in	8 5-in	20	13½
Oklahoma	1916(1929)	29,000	10 14-in	12 5-in	8 5-in	20	13½
Pennsylvania	1916(1931/43)	33,000	12 14-in	12 5-in	8 5-in	21	14
Arizona	1916(1931)	33,000	12 14-in	12 5-in	8 5-in	21	14
Mississippi	1917(1932)	33,000	12 14-in	12 5-in	8 5-in	21	14
New Mexico	1918(1933)	33,000	12 14-in	12 5-in	8 5-in	21	14
Idaho	1919 (1934)	33,000	12 14-in	12 5-in	8 5-in	21	14
Tennessee	1920(1943)	32,000	12 14-in	12 5-in	8 5-in	21	14
California	1921(1944)	32,000	12 14-in	12 5-in	8 5-in	21	14
Maryland	1921	32,000	8 16-in	12 5-in	8 5-in	21	16
Colorado	1923	32,000	8 16-in	12 5-in	8 5-in	21	16
West Virginia	1923(1944)	32,000	8 16-in	12 5-in	8 5-in	21	16

N.B. In ships rebuilt during the war, 5-inch dual-purpose guns replaced the previous secondary and A.A. guns.

Name	Completion year	Tonnage	Main	Secondary		Speed	Armour
Fast battleships							
North Carolina	1941	37,000	9 16-in	20 5-in D.P.		28	12
Washington	1941	37,000	9 16-in	20 5-in D.P.		28	12
South Dakota	1942	37,000	9 16-in	20 5-in D.P.		28	12¼
Indiana	1942	37,000	9 16-in	20 5-in D.P.		28	12¼
Massachusetts	1942	37,000	9 16-in	20 5-in D.P.		28	12¼
Alabama	1942	37,000	9 16-in	20 5-in D.P.		28	12¼
Iowa	1943	46,000	9 16-in	20 5-in D.P.		33	12¼
New Jersey	1943	46,000	9 16-in	20 5-in D.P.		33	12¼
Missouri	1944	46,000	9 16-in	20 5-in D.P.		33	12¼
Wisconsin	1944	46,000	9 16-in	20 5-in D.P.		33	12¼
Alaska	1944	28,000	9 12-in	12 5-in D.P.		33	10½
Guam	1944	28,000	9 12-in	12 5-in D.P.		33	10½

N.B. Perhaps on the principle that it is better to be hung for a lamb than for a sheep or white elephant, the *Alaska* and *Guam* were always described as 'large cruisers'.

Pearl Harbor: a side view of two U.S. battleships moored alongside each other in 'Battleship Row'. The nearest ship, still burning, is the *West Virginia*. Later in the war this vessel was returned to service, but without her characteristic 'waste-paper basket' masts

GERMANY

Old battleships

Schlesien	1908(1927)	12,000	4 11-in	10 5·9-in	4 3·5-in	18	9½
Schleswig-Holstein	1908(1926)	12,000	4 11-in	10 5·9-in	4 3·5-in	18	9½

Special type

Lützow	1933	12,000	6 11-in	8 5·9-in	6 3·9-in	26	2½
Admiral Scheer	1934	12,000	6 11-in	8 5·9-in	6 3·9-in	26	2½
Admiral Graf Spee	1936	12,500	6 11-in	8 5·9-in	6 4·1-in	26	3

Fast battleships

Gneisenau	1938	32,000	9 11-in	12 5·9-in	14 4·1-in	31	14
Scharnhorst	1939	32,000	9 11-in	12 5·9-in	14 4·1-in	31	14
Bismarck	1940	42,000	8 15-in	12 5·9-in	16 4·1-in	29	12½
Tirpitz	1941	42,000	8 15-in	12 5·9-in	16 4·1-in	29	12½

ITALY

Old battleships

Giulio Cesare	1914(1937)	24,000	10 12·6-in	12 4·7-in	8 3·9-in	28	10
Conte di Cavour	1915(1937)	24,000	10 12·6-in	12 4·7-in	8 3·9-in	28	10
Caio Duillio	1915(1940)	24,000	10 12·6-in	12 5·3-in	10 3·6-in	28	10
Andrea Doria	1916(1940)	24,000	10 12·6-in	12 5·3-in	10 3·6-in	28	10

Fast battleships

Vittorio Veneto	1940	41,000	9 15-in	12 6-in	12 3·6-in	30	14
Italia	1940	41,000	9 15-in	12 6-in	12 3·6-in	30	14
Roma	1942	41,000	9 15-in	12 6-in	12 3·6-in	30	14

JAPAN

Old battleships

Kongo	1913(1937)	32,000	8 14-in	14 6-in	8 5-in	30	9
Hiei	1914(1940)	32,000	8 14-in	14 6-in	4 5-in	30	9
Haruna	1915(1934)	32,000	8 14-in	14 6-in	8 5-in	30	9
Kirishima	1915(1936)	32,000	8 14-in	14 6-in	8 5-in	30	9
Fuso	1915(1935)	35,000	12 14-in	14 6-in	8 5-in	24	12
Yamashiro	1917(1935)	35,000	12 14-in	14 6-in	8 5-in	24	12
Ise	1917(1937)	36,000	12 14-in	16 5·5-in	8 5-in	25	12
Hyuga	1918(1934)	36,000	12 14-in	16 5·5-in	8 5-in	25	12
Nagato	1920(1936)	38,000	8 16-in	16 5·5-in	8 5-in	25	11½
Mutsu	1921(1936)	38,000	8 16-in	16 5·5-in	8 5-in	25	11½

Fast battleships

Yamato	1941	65,000	9 18·1-in	12 6·1-in	12 5-in	27	16
Musashi	1942	65,000	9 18·1-in	12 6·1-in	12 5-in	27	16

N.B. The *Hyuga* and *Ise* were converted to 'battleship aircraft carriers' in 1943.

Notes to this table

D.P. signifies a dual-purpose gun. However, most deck-mounted medium weapons had a limited anti-aircraft capacity. Tonnages are 'standard displacement'; some are only approximate, because most navies understated them and only crude corrections can be applied. Speeds are nominal and differ usually from the speeds obtainable under the various conditions of service. Maximum thickness of side armour is only indicative; deck armour and the distribution and extent of armour were equally important.

The German battleship
Tirpitz lies in a Norwegian
fjord beneath floral
camouflage

U-boat attacks, they forced the British navy to maintain powerful
ships to counter them, ships which might have been more profit-
ably used elsewhere. When German battleships were transferred to
Norwegian harbours, Britain was faced with the possibility both of
their breaking out into the North Atlantic and of their attacking
convoys to Russia, and it was not until the *Scharnhorst* and *Tirpitz*
were sunk that these risks disappeared and Britain could transfer
much-needed strength to the East.

Britain's battleships in the first years of the war were employed
in matching those of Germany and Italy. The Italian ships were
unadventurous and played little part in the war; perhaps their main
effect was that in 1942, when Britain was hard-pressed in the East,
the existence of Italian battleships forced Britain to keep in the
Mediterranean battleships which could otherwise have been sent
to contain the Japanese thrust into the Indian Ocean. But by
1943, when Italy surrendered, the Royal Navy's problem was
less a shortage of ships than a shortage of men, and some older
battleships had to be put into reserve so that their crews could be

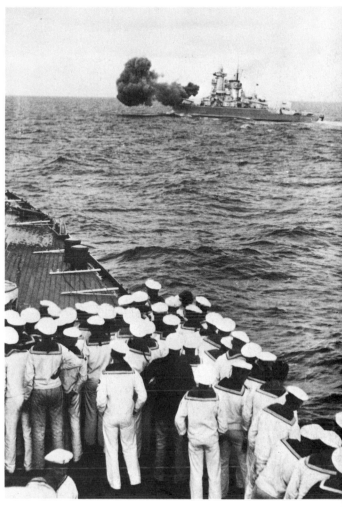

Left: The Japanese battleship *Nagato* undergoes reconstruction in the inter-war period

Right: The crew of a German cruiser watches the pocket battleship *Admiral Scheer* at target practice

used elsewhere. (Another, H.M.S. *Royal Sovereign*, was lent to Russia.) By 1944, with the exception of the four newest ships, Britain's operational battleships were mainly employed in shore bombardment. With air or ground observation, the main armaments of these ships proved immensely destructive, and were of great aid to Allied armies landing in Italy, France, and Holland.

Although at different times and places the French fought both the Allied and the Axis powers, as well as themselves, their battleships played only a small role. After the fall of France in 1940 the British, fearful that French ships in African ports might find their way back to France and then be taken over by Germany, attacked them at Dakar and Oran. Typically described as 'a regrettable necessity', these heavy bombardments against the stationary ships of a recent ally could more accurately be described as an understandable but unproductive panic measure which long soured Anglo-French relations and did not achieve their object. One old battleship was blown up, but the modern *Strasbourg* steamed past the British squadron and reached France safely. Other ships were

not damaged enough to prevent them proceeding to French ports later. In the end, those ships which reached Toulon were scuttled by their crews in 1942, when it seemed that the Germans might indeed commandeer them. Other French ships joined the Allies in 1940 or later. Among them was the new battleship *Richelieu* which, two years after being in action against British battleships, went over to the Free French and served with the British in the East.

Battleships played a relatively small role in the Pacific war. Most of the American Pacific Fleet battleships were put out of action at Pearl Harbor, but this hardly affected the course of the war; the new generation of U.S. battleships was about to come into service and in any case the crucial naval battles were destined to be fought by aircraft carriers. As the war proceeded, the Americans used their new fast battleships as part of carrier task forces, while the older vessels were used for gunfire support of the successive landing operations by the army and marines. The Japanese preferred to cover their carrier forces with detached battleship groups, and their battleships also were used for shore bombardment. There were only two battleship against battleship actions in the Pacific. In one, during the Guadalcanal operations, the

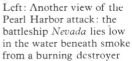

Left: Another view of the Pearl Harbor attack: the battleship *Nevada* lies low in the water beneath smoke from a burning destroyer

Top right: The so-called 'pagoda' masts of Japanese battleships attained the peak of their development in the *Fuso*, shown here on trial in 1933 after reconstruction

Bottom right: The powerful and concentrated anti-aircraft armament of the later U.S. battleships is impressively shown in this picture of U.S.S. *Alabama*

Japanese *Kirishima* confronted the American *Washington* and *South Dakota*. Although the Japanese were better trained in night fighting, the *Washington* had good radar, so although the *South Dakota* was quickly knocked out of the battle the *Washington* was able to overcome the Japanese ship. In the second battleship encounter, during the Leyte Gulf operations of 1944, the two elderly Japanese sister vessels *Fuso* and *Yamashiro*, passing up the Surigao Strait at night, were first attacked by torpedoes and then by a line of old U.S. battleships. The *Fuso* was broken in two by the torpedoes while the *Yamashiro*, after taking four torpedo hits, disappeared in a massive barrage of over 3,000 shells.

In the decades following the war the aircraft carrier and the submarine definitely succeeded the battleship as the main elements of sea power. Other ships, even guided missile ships, were seen as adjuncts to, or defences against, these two types. By the early seventies only the U.S.A. retained battleships, the four *Iowa* vessels being kept in reserve. Four other battleships (the *Texas*, *Massachusetts*, *Alabama* and *North Carolina*) have been kept as floating museums in their respective states. Britain, despite the historic role of her navy in the battleship age, has not preserved any capital ship.

THE YAMATO

In late 1938, in a classic example of how to mislead without actually lying, the Japanese Navy Minister announced that, contrary to Western press rumours, Japan was not building any 40,000- or 50,000-ton battleships. The same press welcomed this statement, but might have felt differently if it had troubled to ask itself what the minister's words actually meant. In fact, Japan was building battleships of the unheard-of displacement of 65,000 tons.

During the twenties and early thirties Japan had adhered to the terms of the Washington Treaty. She had abandoned construction of large battleships started prior to the treaty and contented herself with rebuilding her older types. She had agreed that her navy would be only five-eighths the size of either the British or U.S. navies. But when the treaty came up for renewal Japan felt economically strong enough to build a navy in excess of the former limits. Moreover, militarist groups were stronger, and about to take complete power. For militarists a navy five-eighths the size of each of Japan's potential enemies was not enough. Such a navy might defend Japan against all comers, as it would have the advantage of nearby home bases, but it was not big enough for Japanese expansion.

Thus as early as 1934 design work started on what was to be, and remain, the world's largest battleship. Sixty-three thousand tons was envisaged, partly because this size would cause great embarrassment to the U.S.A.; if the Americans decided to match it they would find themselves with ships too large to pass through the Panama Canal. No fewer than twenty-three alternative designs were drawn and discussed, and more than fifty models given tank tests, before the design was finalized. Then, in 1937, the order for the *Yamato* was placed at the Kure Navy Yard. At about the same time a sister ship, *Musashi*, was ordered from Mitsubishi in Nagasaki. Great secrecy was observed; being an island nation, with foreigners rare and conspicuous, and with an increasingly pervasive security police, such secrecy was not

difficult to impose. To make extra sure, a mile of sisal matting (about 400 tons) was suspended around the *Yamato*'s building slip, causing a temporary and mystifying shortage of this material in Tokyo. To build these ships the building yards had to be enlarged, fitting-out basins deepened, cranes strengthened, and a special ship (also concealed with sisal matting!) had to be built to carry the enormous gun turrets from the manufacturers to the shipyards.

The main armament of the *Yamato* was nine 18·1-inch guns. These, of a size unmatched in any other navy, were the main point of the design; in theory at least no other navy could oppose such ships. The U.S.A. possessed just three battleships, and Britain two, with 16-inch guns, but most of the world's battleships mounted only 14-inch or 15-inch weapons. Even the 16-inch weapons of the new U.S. battleships being built were hardly a match:

Ship	Calibre	Weight of shell (lbs)	Maximum range (miles)
Yamato	18·1-inch	3,200	27
H.M.S. *Nelson*	16-inch	2,000	26
U.S.S. *Colorado*	16-inch	2,100	19
U.S.S. *Washington*	16-inch	2,700	23

The blast from the Japanese guns was devastating, being double that of 16-inch guns. As a result, the ship's boats had to be kept in special blast-proof sheds, and the decking beneath the guns was made of armour plate instead of plain steel. The secondary armament (twelve 6·1-inch guns in triple turrets) was fairly conventional; these guns were not really suitable for anti-aircraft service, whereas the secondary guns of the new British and U.S. battleships were smaller but designed as dual-purpose weapons. For heavy anti-aircraft fire the *Yamato* carried twenty-four 5-inch guns and twenty-four smaller automatic weapons. War experiences later showed that this anti-aircraft defence was too weak and by 1945 six

The Yamato *at sea*

of the 6·1-inch guns had been removed, the weight and space saved being used for more automatic anti-aircraft guns: no fewer than 150 of these 25-mm weapons were then carried.

This ship was probably even more damage-resistant than the German battleships. The hull was divided into almost 1,150 watertight spaces, and its armour protection surpassed that of any other battleship. The side armour had a maximum thickness of sixteen inches. Below the waterline it became thinner, sloping inwards as it descended. This latter feature (first introduced by the British) meant that incoming shells would strike it at a fairly flat angle, thus decreasing their penetrating power. Another idea, not entirely new but first applied successfully in this ship, was the folding inwards of the side armour just above the bottom of the ship, near the magazines. This armour thereby passed, at a thickness of two inches, directly underneath the magazines. As new magnetic torpedoes were designed to explode directly below a ship, rather than on its side, this protection was considered very important. Protection from bombs or plunging shells was provided by an armoured deck, placed rather higher than in other ships. This was nine inches at its maximum thickness. Thirty-three inches below it was a splinter screen designed to catch flying rivets and splinters (similar screens

were placed behind the side armour). The boiler exhaust before entering the funnel passed through a perforated slab of fifteen-inch armour plate, designed to prevent bombs dropping down the funnel into the boiler rooms. The main turret tops were of ten-inch plate (compared to the seven inches of the contemporary U.S.S. *Washington* and the nine inches of H.M.S. *King George V*). The main turret faces were twenty-six inches thick. However, as with other battleships, the secondary turrets were less well armoured, and the possibility of a bomb passing through the turret roof into the secondary magazine was not excluded. But in general the *Yamato* was designed to withstand a one-ton bomb dropped from at least 8,000 feet (a height from which a direct hit was unlikely).

The shape of the hull was unusual in that it broadened out into its full width only in its after half. In common with certain Japanese cruisers, its upper deck was not flat but of wave form; this reflected the wave form of the underlying structure, designed to balance the bending stresses to which the long hull was subject. A bulbous underwater nose was fitted at the stem, decreasing water resistance by about eight per cent. Despite this, the designed speed was only twenty-seven knots. This was less than the new British and U.S. battleships, but even on the 65,000-ton displacement it was not possible to combine 18-inch guns and massive armour with engines more powerful than 150,000 shaft horsepower. In any case, it was no doubt argued that this ship would never have to run away from its enemies.

The *Yamato* was completed in December 1941 and the *Musashi* eight months later. Two further ships were ordered in 1939, of which one (the *Shinano*) was completed as an aircraft carrier; the other was never finished. Historians, interested in Japan's fifty-year effort to become the dominant Pacific sea power, no doubt see a certain symbolism in the fact that its two world-beating battleships entered service in the same year that the Battle of Midway demonstrated that battleships were no longer the key element of naval power.

Neither the *Yamato* nor the *Musashi* ever had the chance to smash British or American battleships, nor indeed to demonstrate the superiority of their 18·1-inch guns. Such actions as they did undertake could equally well have been entrusted to normal size ships. In mid-1942 the *Yamato* was the flagship of the commander-in-chief, Admiral Yamamoto, in the Battle of Midway. Luckily the battleships were kept well in the rear of the aircraft carriers and escaped the U.S. air attacks which proved so catastrophic for the latter. An eyewitness later described how the Admiral, with pallid face and glittering eyes, 'sat sipping rice helplessly' on the bridge of the *Yamato* as the bad news trickled in. In late 1943 the *Yamato* was torpedoed by a U.S. submarine but, being well protected, was not badly damaged. What was perhaps the climax of this battleship's career came in October 1944, in the battles off Leyte Gulf. To attack American ships supporting and supplying the troops which had landed in this part of the Philippines, the Japanese planned an operation involving naval thrusts from three directions. From the north a force of carriers (mainly planeless) were to entice away the covering U.S. heavy ships, while a centre force from the west and a southern force from the south were to pass between the islands and fall upon the undefended U.S. transports and escort carriers. The Japanese centre force centred around the *Yamato*, the *Musashi*, three older battleships, and twelve cruisers. It was commanded by Admiral Kurita, flying his flag in a heavy cruiser. This force,

like the others, was soon spotted by the Americans and came under attack, first by submarines and then by carrier aircraft. The submarines sank two cruisers, including Kurita's flagship. The Admiral then transferred to the *Yamato*. Massive air attacks which followed were countered by anti-aircraft fire, but the Japanese gun defence was not as good as it could have been and the U.S. planes succeeded in sinking the *Musashi* with twenty torpedoes and thirty-three bombs. However, the next morning it appeared that the Japanese plan might come off. Although the *Musashi* had been sunk, and the southern force almost annihilated, the American admiral commanding the fast battleship and

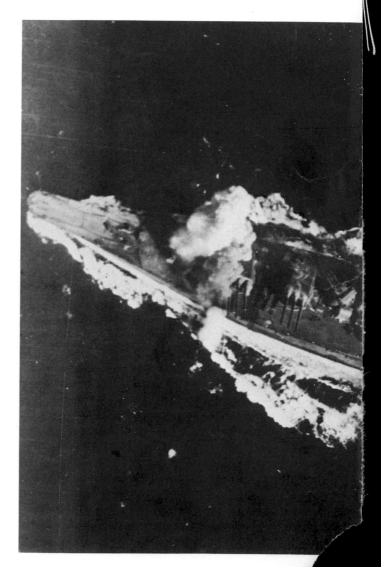

carrier task force (Halsey) had, by a combination of misinformation, miscommunication and misjudgement, allowed himself to be lured from the scene by the Japanese bait of the northern force. Thus when Kurita emerged from the straits into the waters east of the isles he had the surprised U.S. escort carriers in his grasp and would have been able, after sinking them, to destroy the U.S. transports. For the first time since Pearl Harbor the Japanese fleet

seemed to have the Americans at its mercy.

But Kurita, by this time a tired and strained man, spoiled this opportunity. Instead of advancing directly on the almost defenceless carriers he tried to outmanoeuvre them. Gallant attacks by a handful of U.S. destroyers, which torpedoed at least one cruiser, soon disorganized the Japanese. The *Yamato*, after changing course to avoid torpedoes, found herself pursued by six torpedoes which were approaching directly astern and had been set to run, by coincidence, at precisely the *Yamato*'s maximum speed. The battleship, unable without risk to stop, slow down, or turn, was forced to flee from the scene of battle until the torpedoes were spent. This took ten minutes, enough to carry the hapless Kurita too far from the battle to exercise proper control. Only one carrier was sunk by Japanese gunfire, and then the arrival of fresh U.S. aircraft persuaded Kurita to retire. Having accomplished very little and having lost more cruisers, he took the mighty *Yamato* and her consorts back the way they had come. En route, the Japanese air force, hitherto notable mainly for its absence from the battle, made an unsuccessful bombing attack on the long-suffering *Yamato*.

After this inglorious episode the *Yamato* led a quiet life, but in April 1945 she led a Samurai-style attack on the American forces which had landed on Okinawa, perilously close to Japan. Fuel was desperately short by this time, and this force took almost all the supply remaining to Japan. Even so, it was doubted whether the ships would have enough oil to return, so a 'suicide' role was envisaged: the *Yamato* and her consorts would beach themselves and use their heavy guns to bombard the American landing ships and beaches. In the event, the *Yamato* did not need much oil, because she was attacked by U.S. carrier planes before she had moved halfway towards Okinawa. Unprotected by fighters, the *Yamato* and her consorts succumbed to the bombs and torpedoes of almost 400 aircraft. The *Yamato* received, it is thought, ten torpedoes and twenty-three bombs before capsizing and sinking, taking almost 2,500 men down with her. This was the last action of Japanese battleships. The day of the sea-going Samurai was over.

The Yamato's *last battle : one of the 23 bombs which helped to sink her explodes near her fore turret as she vainly tries to reach Okinawa*

THE ADMIRAL GRAF SPEE

Whereas the *Yamato* claims attention by her vast dimensions, the three German 'pocket battleships' aroused interest (and scepticism) by their small size. The *Graf Spee* was the newest of this trio, officially described as 'armoured ships', and became well known all over the world in December 1939 when she was involved in the first major naval action of the war, an action which brought her short but active career to an end.

Although they were not completed until the thirties, these three ships had their origins in the early twenties. The Treaty of Versailles had imposed conditions on Germany which were intended to prevent her resurgence as a great armed power. Her navy was left with no modern capital ships; only pre-Dreadnought battleships like the *Schliesen* and *Schleswig-Holstein* were allowed, and these could not be replaced until they were twenty years old. Their replacements, moreover, were to be of the same size if not smaller: 10,000 tons was the limit imposed by the victorious Allies. Hardly was the ink dry on the treaty when the German naval staff began to devise the best way of utilizing the 10,000-ton limit, their aim being to produce an effective battleship on a displacement less than half that of contemporary foreign battleships. Since at the time it was France, not Britain, which was regarded as the most likely enemy, the new design had to be capable either of fighting or of running away from the strongest French ships, and of destroying lesser vessels. One proposed design was for a ship carrying just four 15-inch guns; by comparison with British battleships, which carried eight guns of this calibre, this was not much, but no French battleship carried guns bigger than 13·4-inch. However, this design was not proceeded with; it was thought that Britain, if not France, would not permit the reintroduction of 15-inch guns in the German navy, and in any case the weight of such guns would have meant that insufficient tonnage would be left to devote to armour and compartmentation. Other proposals were made, all

involving permutations of the three competing qualities sought by all designers: gun-power, protection, and speed. Nothing satisfactory emerged, and in 1923 the project was abandoned for several months. But by the mid-twenties the oldest existing battleships were nearing the end of the twenty-year life fixed for them by the treaty, and it was essential to have a new design to replace them. Thoughts began to turn towards some kind of 'battleship-cruiser', in which speed would receive priority, and eventually a project was adopted which promised a vessel with the protection of a cruiser, a speed somewhat less than a cruiser's but higher than a battleship's, and guns more powerful than a cruiser's although less powerful than a battleship's. Obviously such a design was not going to win spectacular setpiece naval battles, but it would be ideal for commerce raiding, a form of warfare to which a colonial power like France was believed to be vulnerable. The *Deutschland*, the first unit, was ordered in 1928. The design caused some consternation in France and Britain. It had been thought that with a 10,000-ton displacement the best the Germans could achieve would have been simply a modernized form of pre-Dreadnought battleship. Instead, a powerful unit had been evolved. France immediately ordered one of the new battleships which she was allowed under the Washington Treaty; this, the *Dunkerque*, was designed with a speed (twenty-nine knots) high enough to catch the 'pocket battleships' and a main armament (eight 13-inch guns) sufficient to outgun them. The 'pocket battleships' were soon acknowledged to be a triumph of German technology and ingenuity. This triumph was based on three elements: weight-saving techniques, like the use of welding which saved about fifteen per cent of the hull weight; the application of diesel engines; and the understatement of the final displacement which in fact was at least twenty-five per cent greater than the announced displacement of 10,000 tons. The use of diesel instead of steam engines in a warship

of this size was a result of Germany's pre-eminence in this type of motive power. Diesel engines were lighter than steam, and they permitted a much greater range of action for a given stock of fuel. They also produced power, or acceleration, without having to 'raise steam' first. Also, the exhaust fumes were less noticeable than the exhaust from furnaces, an important consideration in ships intended for clandestine operations. The succeeding German battleships, larger and with sophisticated steam engines, were also designed for long range, but were inferior to the 'pocket battleships' in this respect. As the following table shows, even the final generation of British and U.S. battleships could hardly match the *Deutschland* and her two sisters, the *Admiral Scheer* and the *Admiral Graf Spee*:

| | Radius of action (nautical miles): | |
	at 10 knots	at 20 knots
Deutschland (1933)	21,000	10,000
H.M.S. *King George V* (1940)	15,000	6,000
U.S.S. *Iowa* (1943)	14,000	6,000

For ocean raiders, dependent on rare meetings with tankers in secluded waters, the ability to steam long distances without refuelling was an obvious advantage.

Designed for twenty-six knots, all three ships reached twenty-eight knots on trials. There were thus only seven ships in the world which could both out-run them and out-gun them,

The Graf Spee *licking her wounds at Montevideo after the Battle of the River Plate*

the three British battlecruisers and the four Japanese *Kongo* class ships – and neither Britain nor Japan were regarded as potential enemies at this time. The outstanding feature of the design was the gun armament, unprecedented in ships of this size and speed. A triple turret fore and aft each accommodated three 11-inch guns. This calibre, favoured by Germany for its pre-1914 battleships, was chosen partly because the naval staff feared that Britain might intervene to prevent Germany arming her ships with anything bigger: the staff remembered that before 1914 the British had been extremely sensitive to German increases of gun calibre. But this 11-inch gun was an entirely new weapon, far superior to the old 11-inch and far superior, too, to the guns of existing French battleships:

	Weight of shell (lbs)	Maximum range (miles)	Claimed rate of fire (rounds per min.)
Old German 11-inch	670	12	1·5
New German 11-inch	700	26	2·5
French 13·4-inch	1,200	16	2

The greater range of the German gun, together with the high speed of the 'pocket battleships', meant that in theory at least the French battle-

29

ships could be fought successfully, for the higher speed would enable the Germans to keep at a range within the fire of their own guns but too far for the French guns.

Because of weight limitations, the armour could not be heavy. It was designed to offer some protection against the guns of cruisers. Its maximum thickness on the side was $2\frac{1}{2}$ inches and the armoured deck was $1\frac{1}{2}$ inches. The *Graf Spee* had slightly better protection than the first two ships. Her side armour was three inches thick and extended higher, well above the waterline, while the armoured deck was $1\frac{3}{4}$ inches thick and extended the full width of the ship. These improvements were gained at the expense of greater weight (probably totalling about 14,000 tons despite the officially claimed 10,000 tons) and slightly smaller range. But improved engines actually made the *Graf*

Spee slightly faster than her sisters by about half a knot. Both the *Graf Spee* and the *Admiral Scheer* had anti-roll equipment, not fitted in the *Deutschland*. The *Graf Spee* was also notable in that she was the first major ship to be equipped with radar. The aerial of this, resembling a wire mattress, was fitted to the rotating top of the foretop, where it was carefully concealed under a tarpaulin. At this time the German navy was foremost in the development of radar, but was soon overtaken by the British, a circumstance which more than anything else accounted for the British success in hunting down German raiders, both surface ships and submarines.

With her two sisters, the *Graf Spee* played a somewhat less than neutral role in the Spanish Civil War. The *Deutschland* was bombed by the anti-fascists, whereupon the *Scheer* wreaked

vengeance on the inhabitants of the port of Almeria. The *Graf Spee*, however, saw little action at this time. Then, in August 1939, the *Deutschland* and *Graf Spee* were sent separately and secretly into the Atlantic. War against Britain was a distinct possibility, given the German intentions in Poland, and Berlin wished to have its commerce raiders in position right from the start.

It was some days after the outbreak of war that the *Graf Spee* received permission to go into action; apparently Hitler at first hoped that a compromise might be worked out with England and France. For the next two and a half months the *Graf Spee* preyed on shipping, taking nine victims in all (the *Deutschland* took three, before returning home in November; en route for home she was renamed *Lützow*, apparently because of the psychological effect

which was feared, should she be sunk while bearing a name so dear to sentimental German hearts). The *Graf Spee*'s nine victims did not make a very imposing catch: a single U-boat would probably have done better. On the other hand her activity caused widespread alarm and obliged the British and French navies to form hunting groups at a time when their ships and energies were in demand elsewhere.

Making occasional rendezvous with her supply ship *Altmark*, from which she took supplies and oil and to which she transferred prisoners, the *Graf Spee* moved quietly from the north

After scuttling, the Graf Spee *burned for several days in the shallow waters off Montevideo. Inset : Results of the British cruisers' gunfire : the* Graf Spee's *damaged hull and burned-out aircraft*

It had been hoped to power these ships with diesel engines, but these were still unavailable in the size needed. Instead, a very sophisticated high-pressure steam turbine system was adopted. Working at 735 lbs per square inch, the boilers were very efficient, but demanded careful maintenance. The designed speed was thirty-two knots, although the achieved speed was probably only thirty-one. Over 6,000 tons of oil could be carried, giving a range (at an economical cruising speed of seventeen knots) of about 10,000 miles. The main armament of nine 11-inch guns was in the classic arrangement of two triple turrets forward and another aft. The secondary armament (twelve 5·9-inch guns) was arranged conventionally on each side of the superstructure.

Even though for much of the war the *Scharnhorst* and *Gneisenau* operated together, it was the former which had by far the liveliest record, seeing more action than any other German surface ship. In November 1939 the pair approached Iceland and encountered the British armed merchant cruiser *Rawalpindi*, one of several enforcing the distant blockade of Germany. Unarmoured, high-sided, lightly armed, the *Rawalpindi* advanced to fight the *Scharnhorst*, managing to score one hit before being sent to the bottom. Fearing that this action would have given time for other British ships to take up intercepting positions, the two German ships abandoned their intention of breaking out into the Atlantic shipping routes. In spring 1940 the pair covered the German invasion of Norway, which can be regarded as the German navy's most successful operation. In the face of Britain's superior sea power, the German navy succeeded in putting ashore the first waves of invading troops and then keeping them supplied, but at a cost in cruisers and destroyers which virtually made the operation unrepeatable. The *Scharnhorst* and the *Gneisenau* encountered the British battlecruiser *Renown* in this campaign. Although they could probably have destroyed this ship (whose destroyer escorts could not keep up in the heavy seas) the German commander chose to retire, but not before the *Scharnhorst* had received several hits. During the Allied evacuation of Norway the pair sank a tanker and an empty

troopship and then came upon the British aircraft carrier *Glorious*, escorted by only two destroyers. Again it was the *Scharnhorst* which saw most of the action. The *Glorious* was soon sunk, but in an extraordinary contest the last surviving destroyer (the *Acasta*) managed just before sinking to score a hit with a torpedo. This forced the Germans to return to port; if they had continued they would probably have encountered a convoy, as well as a cruiser carrying the King of Norway to Britain.

After repairs lasting four months, the *Scharnhorst*, still with the *Gneisenau*, broke out into the North Atlantic and the pair sank twenty-two ships before taking refuge in Brest, from where they could threaten the British with more sorties against the shipping routes. Massive bombing attacks were made on them over almost a year by the R.A.F., which succeeded in flattening Brest but inflicted little important damage on the German raiders. However, these bombing attacks did make Brest unsuitable as a base. There followed the famous 'Channel dash' (see p.108) in which the pair, plus the cruiser *Prinz Eugen*, succeeded in returning to Germany via the Straits of Dover. But both battleships were damaged by mines off Holland during this exploit; the *Gneisenau*, attacked by bombers when in dry dock, never returned to service, but the *Scharnhorst* was repaired and sent to Norway. Here she did nothing, but her presence was a costly embarrassment to the British, who had to make elaborate covering arrangements for the Russian convoys. When eventually the *Scharnhorst* was allowed actually to attack one of these convoys in late 1943, she was intercepted on her first sortie and sunk by H.M.S. *Duke of York* at the Battle of North Cape. Thus ended the career of the German navy's most successful surface ship. (For more details of the *Scharnhorst*'s last battle, see the index entry 'North Cape'.)

THE BISMARCK

It was only to be expected that the *Scharnhorst* and *Gneisenau* would not by themselves satisfy the German naval staff, especially as under the Anglo-German Naval Agreement three additional battleships of 35,000 tons were permissible. Design work had begun as early as 1932 on large modern battleships, and the resulting plans were brought up to date. A late revision of the plans was occasioned by the staff's realization that the arrangement for aircraft stowage and catapulting was inferior to the British system introduced in certain rebuilt battleships. This system, with the catapult running right across the ship abaft the funnel, was incorporated in the final design for a ship which would ostensibly be of 35,000 tons. Two ships, the *Bismarck* and the *Tirpitz*, were laid down in 1935 and 1936 respectively.

Eight 15-inch guns were mounted. These were of a new type, considered to be the equal of older 16-inch guns in other navies. The secondary armament was twelve 5·9-inch weapons, mounted in side turrets. An anti-aircraft battery of sixteen 4·1-inch dual-purpose guns was also carried. High-pressure steam turbines were designed to produce 138,000 shaft horsepower and a speed of twenty-nine knots, but on trials produced enough power for more than thirty knots. The side armour was sixteen feet deep, and at its thickest was twelve inches. The armoured deck was five inches thick at its strongest part, and this was supplemented by an armoured upper deck two inches thick. Following the habitual practice of German naval architecture, the division of the ships into strong watertight compartments was extremely thorough; although German propaganda claims that these ships were 'unsinkable' were obviously false, there is little doubt that they were considerably less sinkable than the battleships of other countries.

After completion in 1940, the *Bismarck* worked up to full efficiency in the Baltic, the traditional training ground of the German navy in wartime. In 1941 a big Atlantic operation was envisaged, with the *Scharnhorst* and *Gneisenau* moving into the Atlantic from Brest and drawing away the British battleships, thus enabling the *Bismarck* to enter the Atlantic from the north and devastate the British convoys. However, the British air attacks on Brest forestalled this plan. Despite the misgivings of the German admiral commanding, Lutjens, it was nevertheless decided to send the *Bismarck*, with the cruiser *Prinz Eugen*, into the Atlantic in May. The former was to lure away the British heavy ships covering the convoys, and the latter would then attack those convoys.

Thanks to British intelligence in Scandinavia, and sporadic air observation, the departure of the German ships was known to the British Admiralty. In the Denmark Strait, between Iceland and Greenland, the British cruisers

Suffolk and *Norfolk* discovered and shadowed the raiders. The *Suffolk*, unknown to the Germans, was equipped with a new and powerful type of radar. The only heavy ships near and fast enough to intercept the Germans were H.M.S. *Hood* and H.M.S. *Prince of Wales*. The former was old and had never been rebuilt with better armour, while the latter was so new that she had not reached full efficiency (she still had civilian fitters and technicians on board in case of trouble). When these two ships met the Germans early in the morning of 24 May their angle of approach put them at a considerable disadvantage: whereas the German ships could use their full broadsides the British could bring to bear only their forward guns. Moreover, only the forward British range-finders could be used, for the same reason, and these were hampered by flying spray. Gunfire began at 5.53 a.m., the *Bismarck* firing at the *Hood* with her main guns and at the *Prince of*

Wales with her secondary armament. At 6.01 a.m. the *Hood* was struck by a shell which penetrated a magazine. She blew up and disappeared within about three minutes; of her complement of 1,441 men only three were picked up. The *Prince of Wales* soon began to suffer, both from the fire of the two German ships and from mechanical defects in her main guns; her captain wisely decided to break off the action behind a smokescreen. But the *Prince of Wales*, despite her troubles, had succeeded in damaging the *Bismarck*: one shell had damaged the latter's fuel supply and another had flooded a boiler room, reducing her speed by about two knots. Because of this damage Admiral Lutjens decided to abandon the Atlantic foray: the *Bismarck* would make for a French port while the *Prinz Eugen* alone

The Bismarck *soon after commissioning, in 1940*

would proceed against the British convoys.

Meanwhile the British Admiralty was bringing up all available ships. Aircraft from the carrier *Victorious*, another new and unprepared ship, succeeded in scoring one torpedo hit against the *Bismarck*'s side armour, but this did little damage. Soon afterwards the shadowing cruisers lost touch and for more than a day the British had little idea where the *Bismarck* was heading. A radio fix made when the Germans unwisely broke radio silence to communicate with their superiors was wrongly interpreted on the British flagship and for some hours the main British forces moved in the wrong direction. But on 26 May an R.A.F. flying boat spotted the *Bismarck* about 700 miles west of Brest.

The British heavy ships were not in a position to overtake their quarry without risking an entry into waters covered by German bombers. Moreover, fuel was short: the *Prince of Wales* had already been forced for this reason to abandon the chase. Luckily the aircraft carrier *Ark Royal*, despatched from Gibraltar, was in striking distance of the German battleship, and her Swordfish torpedo bombers scored two hits. One of the torpedoes damaged the Achilles' heel of all battleships, the steering, and this was decisive. Unable to steer a straight course, her speed reduced, shadowed through the night by cruisers and destroyers, the *Bismarck* was confronted next morning by the battleships H.M.S. *Rodney* and H.M.S. *King George V*. An early shot struck the control tower, killing key officers and dislocating the fire control system. After this the *Bismarck*'s gunfire became inaccurate and the British could safely close the range. After one hour and fifty minutes of action the *Bismarck* sank. Only about 115 of her crew were picked up by the British, who did not linger to look for more in case U-boats were in the vicinity. Admiral Lutjens was among the 1,977 who died.

The *Bismarck*'s sister, the *Tirpitz*, had a longer career. A planned operation in the Atlantic with a 'pocket battleship' in late 1941 was called off, and the battleship spent most of her life anchored in Norwegian fiords. A foray against a convoy to Russia was frustrated by disturbing though inaccurate air attacks from the

carrier H.M.S. *Victorious*. On the other hand, a British belief that she was about to attack the convoy P.Q.17 led to the dispersal and destruction of most of that convoy by aircraft and submarines. The presence of this ship was always a threat to communications: from Norway the battleship might attack the Russian convoys or slip out into the Atlantic. The British therefore made great efforts to destroy her. Both British and Russian bombers attacked her from bases in Russia, British midget submarines damaged her with underwater charges, Fleet Air Arm bombers put her out of action for several more months. Finally R.A.F. bombers, using special five-ton bombs, managed to capsize her in late 1944.

The *Tirpitz* was the last battleship that Germany built, and is regarded by Germans as the finest battleship which any country ever designed. Certainly she and her sister could absorb great punishment, and it is true that, like their predecessors, this pair was designed and built with great ingenuity. Yet they had their weaknesses. In several respects the armour distribution was old-fashioned. Horizontal protection was insufficient and moreover (unlike the new British battleships) vital communication lines were placed above the armoured deck. In the *Bismarck*'s final engagement, these exposed lines were soon cut. Also, the secondary armament, with only 35-degree elevation, could hardly be used against aircraft. The French *Dunkerque*, laid down as early as 1931, had a dual-purpose secondary armament, and so did the *Bismarck*'s British and U.S. contemporaries. The absence of suitable dual-purpose guns meant that the German ships carried three sets of guns, main, secondary, and anti-aircraft, instead of two, and moreover the anti-aircraft armament was not especially strong. It is strange that German designers, so adept at making the best possible use of available space and tonnage, should have failed to exploit the possibility of a dual-purpose secondary armament.

Admiral Golovko, who commanded the Soviet Northern Fleet and whose biggest ship was a destroyer, wrote in his diary that the *Duke of York*, which he visited at Murmansk, had made 'a powerful impression' on him. He was especially impressed by the ship's bakery, and took a sackful of buns home with him. This was a rare visit for a British battleship, because only the smaller escorts of the Russian convoys usually went right through to Murmansk. The distant escorts, based on Iceland, usually followed about 200 miles behind the convoys, and turned back as soon as it became certain that the German heavy units based in northern Norway were not going to intervene because of the reluctance in Berlin to risk losing ships. In Golovko's words, the Germans left harbour 'once a year by special permission'.

Covering the Russian convoys and, later, covering carrier operations off Norway, were the *Duke of York*'s main activities in the war. Completed in late 1941 as the third of the *King George V* class battleships, she took Churchill to America while working up, and then until late 1944 operated in northern waters. The climax of her career was on Boxing Day of 1943, when she encountered the German battleship *Scharnhorst* at the Battle of North Cape.

The German naval staff, with some hesitation, had given permission for the *Scharnhorst* to attack a Russian convoy, and she sailed with a destroyer escort from her refuge in the Altenfiord on Christmas Day. Her foray had been half expected by the British, who had made appropriate dispositions. Located and harried by cruisers and separated from his destroyers, the German commander Admiral Bey retreated directly towards the *Duke of York* which, unknown to the Germans, was approaching with a cruiser and four destroyers. Lacking radar as effective as that of the British, the Germans were completely surprised when, in the Arctic darkness, the *Scharnhorst* was suddenly illuminated by British starshells. The *Duke of York* opened fire at 12,000 yards, and soon put one of the *Scharnhorst*'s turrets out of action. An attempt to escape northwards was frustrated by the British cruisers and soon the *Scharnhorst* was slowed down by more hits from the *Duke of York*. The *Duke of York* was hit several times, but not seriously. A hit on her mast did break a vital connection with the radar gunnery control, but this was soon put right by an officer who climbed the mast to rejoin the loose ends. An hour and a half after the *Duke of York* first opened fire, the *Scharnhorst*'s last main turret fell silent; its commander had already signalled to Hitler a 'fight to the last shell' message. British destroyers renewed their torpedo attacks and after another eighty-five minutes the German battleship sank, leaving only thirty-six survivors. By this time the *Duke of York* had fired nearly 450 14-inch shells and nearly 700 5·25-inch.

This was the last attack by German surface ships on the Russian convoys, but until the *Tirpitz* was dealt with the *Duke of York* was still needed in northern waters. Finally, in 1944 she went for refit and then to the Far East, where she arrived in time to participate in the Japanese surrender in Tokyo Bay on 2 September 1945.

The *Duke of York* and her sister *King George V* were the most successful of the five battleships completed by Britain during the war. These five (the *King George V*, *Prince of Wales*, *Duke of York*, *Howe* and *Anson*) were of a much-criticized design. They had been laid down at a time when Britain was still hoping to persuade other nations to limit future construction to 35,000 tons and future guns to 14-inch calibre. Thus while Germany, Italy, and France were building battleships with 15-inch guns, the U.S.A. with 16-inch, and Japan (secretly) with 18-inch, Britain's navy was provided with what seemed to be an inferior weapon. In partial compensation the *King George V* class was provided with ten main guns as against the eight of the French and German ships and the nine of the U.S., Italian and Japanese. To permit this number, an unusual and untried arrangement of turrets was adopted. There was a quadruple turret fore and aft, with a smaller

two-gun turret superfiring forward. Moreover, the British public was assured that the new 14-inch gun was more effective than the old 15-inch – this may have been true, but the public relations men did not add that the *new* 15-inch guns of the Germans were likewise superior to the old British 15-inch:

		Shell weight (lbs)	Range (miles)	Claimed rounds per minute
New British	14-in	1,550	23	2
Old British	15-in	1,920	20	2
New French	15-in	1,960	27	2
New German	15-in	1,750	22	3
New Italian	15-in	1,940	26	1·5

However, it could be argued that the longer range of the heavier calibres was only useful in clear weather, and that British ships were most likely to fight at close ranges in the poorer visibility of northern waters. The *Duke of York*'s action with the *Scharnhorst*, which commenced at 12,000 yards, and the *Prince of Wales*'s earlier fight with the *Bismarck*, which was close enough to enable the secondary guns to be used, seem to justify this argument.

In other respects the *King George V* class, despite criticism, seems to have been a very competent design, bearing in mind the tonnage

One of a series of official photographs taken of the Duke of York *soon after completion. The unusual quadruple turret is clearly visible*

limitation (which was actually exceeded, but not by much, until new wartime equipment raised the displacement to about 38,000 tons). The secondary armament of sixteen 5·25-inch guns suitable for both air and surface targets made the best possible use of the space and weight made available for it. The designed speed of twenty-seven knots was a little slower than contemporary foreign battleships, although in practice twenty-nine knots could be reached. But certain defects, already anticipated by some, became very evident in the Battle of North Cape. Like other British battleships, the *Duke of York* tended to dive under rather than ride heavy seas. Thus in intercepting the *Scharnhorst* the *Duke of York* literally ploughed ahead at only seventeen knots, and even at that low speed seawater cascaded down the ventilators. Also, when her after turret fired on its extreme forward bearing, searing gases from the barrels flashed down nearby ventilators and into the wardroom, gutting that compartment. Fortunately, because of 'Action Stations', it was empty at the time.

U.S.S. ALABAMA

One of the several achievements of American shipbuilders was to reduce construction time to unprecedentedly brief periods. Thus U.S.S. *Alabama* was laid down at Norfolk Navy Yard in February 1940 and was ready in August 1942, a building time of only thirty months (compared to four years for the contemporary *King George V* and *Bismarck*). If it be true that a warship is obsolete before it is completed, a short building time at least reduces the degree of obsolescence. Certainly, the *Alabama* and her three sisters (the *South Dakota*, *Indiana* and *Massachusetts*) were regarded as highly successful ships when they joined the fleet during the first difficult year of war. After the war the *Alabama* and the *Massachusetts* were acquired by their adoptive states and preserved as memorials.

They had been preceded by the *Washington* and the *North Carolina* which, although carrying the same nine 16-inch guns, were less advanced in their design. The *Alabama* and her sisters were notable in that their hull armour was carried internally. The outer plating was regarded as only very light protection and behind it on each side of the ship were three longitudinal bulkheads with ample space between them to cushion the explosions of shells or torpedoes. Behind the innermost bulk-

head was the main side armour, inclined outwards at an angle of nineteen degrees to flatten the angle of impact of incoming shells. This armour was twelve inches thick at its strongest part, tapering below the waterline to one inch. There was a triple bottom beneath the engines and magazines and this feature, together with the total of six longitudinal bulkheads, made external anti-torpedo bulges unnecessary. Horizontal protection was provided by two armoured decks above the most vital parts, together amounting to six inches in places. The steering compartment was given exceptionally good protection, with 8-inch plate above and 13-inch at the sides. Compared with the preceding class, the engines and boilers were packed into a small space, so that the area requiring maximum thickness of armour was reduced; this in turn enabled the general armour area to be extended. Concentration of the boilers led to a concentration of the superstructure, clearly seen in photographs; this gave the anti-aircraft guns a better field of fire. The anti-aircraft armament was in any case exceptionally strong; the twenty 5-inch dual-purpose guns, available for use against approaching or high-flying aircraft, could each fire ten rounds per minute, while the ninety 20-mm and 40-mm automatic guns provided short-range cover.

With their twenty-eight knots, these ships were suitable for fast carrier task forces, and for much of the war this was their role. The *Alabama* and a sister ship, however, served with the British

U.S.S. Alabama *just before she joined forces with the British fleet in 1943*

The stern of the Alabama, *showing her aftermost automatic anti-aircraft guns and one of her reconnaissance float planes beneath the aircraft-handling crane*

fleet for a few months in 1943; H.M.S. *Malaya* had been withdrawn from active service because of advancing senility and the U.S. battleships were required to strengthen the defence of North Atlantic and Russian convoys. But by the end of 1943 the *Alabama* was in the Pacific, covering the carriers and bombarding the succession of islands which were assaulted by the U.S. marines and army. In June 1944 she took part in the Battle of the Philippine Sea but, as this battle was conducted by aircraft, only her anti-aircraft armament came into action. Later in 1944 the *Alabama* took part in the Battle for Leyte Gulf but, being part of Admiral Halsey's force, she was marched 300 miles to the north and then 300 miles to the south without sighting the enemy. After this excitement she reverted to her old role, taking part in the carrier attacks on Okinawa and Formosa. In July and August 1945, with four other battleships, she bombarded targets in Japan itself. Japan, with her navy mostly sunk, with no oil for the surviving ships, and with her air force short of planes and crews,

could do little to resist these attacks. Near Tokyo, the Hitachi industrial area was bombarded. Over 1,600 16-inch shells were fired, with devastating results. Afterwards the Japanese inhabitants said that they found naval bombardments far more terrifying than aerial bombing. Although air force cynics may have claimed that this was because the navy was more likely to hit civilian targets by mistake, the truth is that the flat trajectory and high velocity of naval shells, together with the absence of warning of their approach, and their greater accuracy after the first few salvoes, did make them a more destructive, and frightening, and economical, weapon against coastal targets. That is why in 1968 the U.S.S. *New Jersey* was taken out of mothballs and sent to bombard targets in Vietnam.

U.S.S. WASHINGTON

Of the twenty-seven U.S. battleships which took part in the war, it is difficult to select those one or two which were outstanding. The U.S. Navy had no battleship like the German *Scharnhorst* or the British *Warspite*, a battleship repeatedly in the headlines. This was mainly because the battleship was not the prime warship in the Pacific campaign; the American equivalent of the *Scharnhorst* and *Warspite* was not a battleship, but the aircraft carrier *Enterprise*. Nevertheless, the U.S.S. *Washington* deserves notice, for at one crucial stage of the war she was the only modern battleship available in the Pacific, and later she distinguished herself in one of those ship-against-ship encounters which occurred so often in naval theory but so rarely in the Pacific war.

The U.S.A. was the last of the naval powers to start new battleship construction in the thirties, and the *Washington* and her sister *North Carolina* were the first of the American fast battleships. The *Washington* was begun at the Philadelphia Navy Yard in 1938 and completed in May 1941. The design was influenced by a reluctance to introduce ships which might seem to weaken America's support for further treaty limitations of battleship size. However, unlike the British, the Americans did not design their new ships around the 14-inch gun, although this was the calibre they had recommended as the future maximum. Instead, these and subsequent U.S. battleships mounted nine 16-inch guns in three triple turrets. It was fear of what Japan might be doing which determined the choice of the larger weapon, and in the light of later knowledge it would seem that this was a sensible decision. Nevertheless, it was decided that the tonnage should not seem excessive, and since armour had a high priority it was speed (that is, boiler power) which was sacrificed to permit a nominal displacement of 35,000 tons. The real displacement was a little more than this, which meant that the 121,000 S.H.P. engines could produce a maximum speed of 28 knots, compared to the 33 knots of the later and bigger *Iowa* class.

A narrow belt of waterline armour, which did not extend to the forward part of the ship, was 12 inches thick and inclined at 17 degrees. What was considered to be a very vulnerable part of a warship, the steering compartment, was exceptionally well protected with 12-inch sides and 6-inch ceiling. For protection against underwater explosions, the hull had bulges and a triple bottom. To reduce weight, electric welding was extensively employed, and the hull was strengthened by the elimination of all portholes. The aircraft were positioned at the stern but were not provided with a hangar as in contemporary U.S. cruisers, apparently because of the danger of internal fires resulting from damaged fuel tanks.

In early 1942 the *Washington* began her active service with the British Home Fleet. This move was indirectly connected with the war against Japan; a Japanese invasion of Madagascar was feared, so a pre-emptive Allied landing was made to take over this Vichy French island which occupied such a strategic position off southern Africa. The British ships sent from Gibraltar to support the invasion were replaced by units sent from Scapa Flow, and to replace the latter the *Washington*, the aircraft carrier *Wasp*, and two cruisers were sent across the Atlantic. En route, the admiral commanding this force was washed overboard from the *Washington* in heavy seas, and the plane sent by the *Wasp* to search for him was also lost.

The main role of the *Washington* in this period was to provide distant cover for the convoys to Russia, but after a few months she was transferred to the Pacific. Her sister *North Carolina* was already there, and on 15 September 1942 became a victim of one of the most remarkable submarine successes of the war. The Japanese submarine *I-19* sighted an American task force and fired six long-range torpedoes. Three of these hit the *Wasp*, which never reached port, and three passed under or near a destroyer. These three torpedoes continued for another five miles and ran into another U.S. task force. One torpedo irreparably damaged a destroyer, and another blew a 32 ft × 18 ft hole in the *North*

Carolina. The latter went for repair, leaving the *Washington* as the only modern Allied battleship in the Pacific.

Subsequently the *Washington* was joined by the new *South Dakota*, and this pair took part in the four-day Battle of Guadalcanal. An intense struggle raged on this south Pacific island, and every night the Japanese navy sent fast warships, the so-called 'Tokyo Express', to bombard American positions and to bring supplies and reinforcements to the Japanese troops. The fate of the struggle obviously depended on sea communications, and both contenders thought they had enough ships in the area to win. There was no question of either side withdrawing its ships to await more favourable circumstances. At the Battle of Savo Island in August 1942 the Japanese had won local naval superiority, which they only partially lost at the Battle of Cape Esperance in October. These two cruiser engagements were followed in October by the Battle of Santa Cruz, in which the carrier U.S.S. *Hornet* was sunk and the carrier *Enterprise* saved only by good luck and the anti-aircraft batteries of the *South Dakota*. The *Washington*, temporarily detached from this carrier group, was lucky to escape the torpedoes of a Japanese submarine.

On 13 November an American cruiser and destroyer force met the Japanese night bombardment detachment and reduced the battleship *Hiei* to sinking condition, but lost two of its cruisers. The following night the Japanese sent in the *Hiei*'s sister *Kirishima* and two heavy cruisers to bombard American land targets, especially the vital Henderson airfield on which the Americans depended for local air supremacy. To meet this Japanese force Admiral Lee, one of the most intelligent of U.S. admirals, took his flagship *Washington*, the *South Dakota*, and four destroyers to a position west of Guadalcanal. A Japanese light cruiser, leading the enemy's destroyer screen, was picked up by the *Washington*'s radar at nine miles. When the cruiser was in visual range, the battleship opened fire, but no hits were scored before the target retreated. The Japanese commander had split his force into four groups. This made it almost impossible for him to control the course of the coming engagement, but it confused the American radar operators, who found contacts in all directions.

Soon after 2300 the opposing destroyer screens made contact, and in the ensuing battle all four of the U.S. destroyers were crippled or sunk despite supporting fire from the battleships. At a critical point the *South Dakota*'s power failed for a few minutes, long enough for that battleship's radar operators to lose track of events. At about the same time, blast from her guns ignited her aircraft, stowed on deck at the stern. Fortunately, further blast toppled the blazing aircraft overboard.

The Japanese destroyers, having dealt with the U.S. destroyers, soon sighted the troubled

46

South Dakota. They launched thirty-four torpedoes, but none of these hit their target. The approaching Japanese heavy ships held their fire until they were within 5,000 yards of the unsuspecting *South Dakota.* Then they opened their searchlight shutters and blazed away. In a few minutes the *South Dakota* received forty-two hits and seemed doomed.

Meanwhile the *Washington* had been ploughing through a sea populated with survivors of the

U.S.S. Washington. *Fighter aircraft (Hurricanes) of H.M.S.* Victorious *in the foreground*

sunken U.S. destroyers. Her radar had been tracking the *Kirishima* and the two Japanese heavy cruisers but fire had been withheld because it was thought that one or other of the apparent targets might have been the *South Dakota.* This doubt was resolved as soon as the Japanese opened fire, at which time the *Washington* was only 8,000 yards away. In their preoccupation with the *South Dakota*, the Japanese had not noticed the approach of this second U.S. battleship. One of the *Washington*'s 5-inch guns began to fire starshell to illuminate the target, and the 16-inch guns and some of the 5-inch fired at the *Kirishima* while the remaining 5-inch weapons occupied themselves with the cruisers *Atago* and *Takao.* Under this cover the *South Dakota* was able to extricate herself. In about seven minutes of combat the *Washington* fired seventy-five 16-inch shells. Nine of these, together with about forty 5-inch shells, found their target in the devastated *Kirishima*, which later had to be sunk by her accompanying destroyers. Thus for the second successive night the Japanese bombarding force had lost a battleship.

After dealing with the *Kirishima* the *Washington*, undamaged, moved out to sea to draw away the Japanese destroyers from the damaged American ships. She succeeded in this so well that several torpedoes were directed at her, but these detonated prematurely in the turbulence of her wake. The *South Dakota* was later repaired in the U.S.A.

Later in the war the *Washington*, like her sister *North Carolina*, supported the aircraft carriers in the successive amphibious operations against Japanese-held islands. The fast battleships' major role was to provide anti-aircraft cover for the carriers (by the end of the war the *Washington* mounted, apart from her twenty dual-purpose 5-inch guns, sixty 28mm automatic anti-aircraft weapons). The heavy guns were used in shore bombardment, but had no chance of action in the Battle for Leyte Gulf, in which the *Washington* was part of Admiral Halsey's force.

After the war the *Washington* was soon decommissioned, and was scrapped in 1961. Her sister was luckier, being acquired by North Carolina for permanent exhibition at Wilmington.

H.M.S. WARSPITE

Of all Britain's battleships, the *Warspite* was regarded with the greatest affection. Possibly this was because she got into so many scrapes (throughout her long career she was subject to sudden jamming of the rudder, and in the First World War twice collided with sister ships), or perhaps it was because she took part in so many successful actions. She was the second oldest of the battleships, and her age began to tell towards the end of the war; in fact she was withdrawn from operations before the war ended.

She was launched in 1913 by Devonport Dockyard in the presence of the First Lord of the Admiralty, Winston Churchill. She was the second ship of the *Queen Elizabeth* class (the others were the *Valiant*, *Barham* and *Malaya*). This design can be regarded as the culmination of the naval race with Germany, and the *Queen Elizabeth* and her sisters were the first to carry 15-inch guns and to be fired entirely by oil. With their unprecedentedly heavy armament of eight 15-inch and sixteen 6-inch guns, these ships were a great reinforcement for the Grand Fleet in the First World War, and their value was enhanced by their twenty-four knots speed, three knots faster than preceding designs. At the Battle of Jutland the *Warspite's* guns damaged the German battlecruisers, but then her rudder jammed, causing her to circle under the German guns. She was badly damaged and had to withdraw.

Some of the damage received at Jutland was patched only temporarily, but many of these temporary repairs lasted until the mid-thirties, when the *Warspite*, the *Queen Elizabeth* and the *Valiant* were rebuilt. They returned to service completely altered: virtually only their hulls and heavy guns were left unchanged. A compact control tower replaced the old bridge structure, more anti-aircraft weapons were fitted, and these had a better arc of fire because only one quite small funnel was needed. Extra deck armour was fitted as protection against bombs and plunging shells.

In 1939 the *Warspite* was part of the Mediter-
ranean Fleet, but she was soon transferred to the Home Fleet. She became one of several battleships protecting Atlantic convoys from surface raiders. In 1940 she was used in the Norway campaign and was the key factor in the Second Battle of Narvik. Here, with nine destroyers, she sailed up a long and narrow fiord to destroy eight German destroyers. Then she returned to the Mediterranean in anticipation of Italian entry into the war. Soon after Italy's declaration of war, the *Warspite* took part in the action off Calabria, in which her guns damaged an Italian battleship. For most of the year 1940–41 she was used as cover for convoys, with oc-

H.M.S. Warspite, *photographed near the end of her active career*

casional spells bombarding shore targets in North Africa and Greece in support of the army. In March 1941, still as Admiral Cunningham's flagship, she was one of three battleships which, benefiting from new radar, surprised and sank three Italian heavy cruisers in the night action off Cape Matapan.

A few weeks later, while helping in the evacuation of troops from Crete, she was heavily bombed by German aircraft. About 400 bombs were aimed at her, but by violent manoeuvring she evaded all but one. However, this one penetrated the deck and caused serious damage. She was sent via Suez and the Pacific to the U.S.A. for repair. After this she reinforced the weak British fleet facing the Japanese in the Indian Ocean, before returning to the Mediterranean. For the remainder of her career she was used for shore bombardment in support of British and U.S. troops. In the Italian campaign she was attacked by glider bombs. One of these exploded in a boiler room, blowing out part of the ship's bottom. Power and light were cut off, and lack of forced ventilation made the ship almost uninhabitable for the three days needed to withdraw to a safe port; in those three days the crew consumed about 3,000 gallons of lime juice but few felt like eating solid food. She returned to Britain, but before repairs were complete she was used to provide gunfire support for the Normandy landings. When returning to Britain to replace her worn gun barrel linings she was badly damaged by a mine. Once again she was repaired and in November 1944 carried out her last operation, the bombardment of Walcheren.

After three years in reserve, the *Warspite* was sold for scrap. But right to the end she maintained her reputation as a capricious ship. While being towed to the breakers, she broke loose and in a 60-m.p.h. gale wedged herself ashore on the Cornish rocks. Here she remained, and it took almost ten years for the ship breakers to dismantle her.

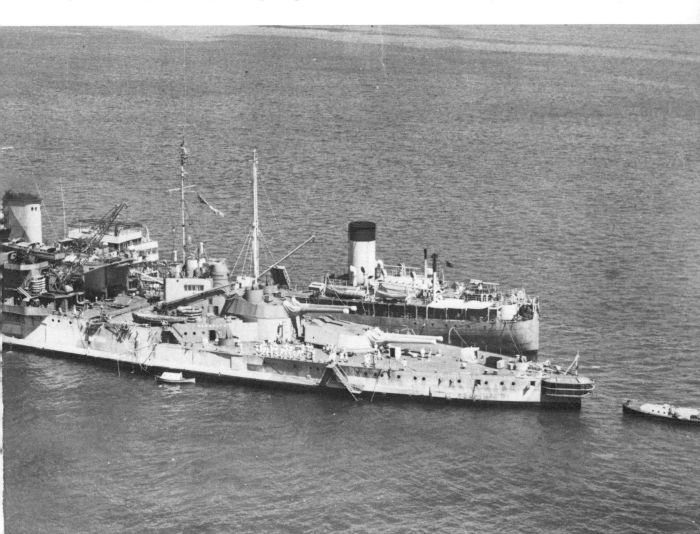

U.S.S. TEXAS

In the Pacific war the battleship played a subsidiary role, supporting either the aircraft carriers or the soldiers. There were only two battleship versus battleship encounters, and these were both confused night actions. No American battleship therefore had the opportunity to win the kind of fame which the *Bismarck* or the *Warspite* acquired. U.S.S. *Texas* features here partly because she is the only U.S. 'battlewagon' of pre-1914 design to survive to the present day, and partly because her wartime activities, while not celebrated, were certainly extensive (she steamed 124,000 miles during the war).

Reference to the table on p. 18 will show that during the First World War the U.S.A. was building a fleet of Dreadnoughts which was easily a match for other navies. Beginning with the *New York* and the *Texas* of 1914, and ending with the *California*, ordered in 1915, eleven battleships were built, having the same general characteristics and able therefore to operate effectively as one squadron without any embarrassing difference of speed, manoeuvrability or gun range. In the final years of that war, with the slogan of 'a navy second to none', a new series of even more powerful ships, this time armed with 16-inch guns, was planned. But thanks to the Washington Treaty only three of these were built.

The characteristic feature of these U.S. designs was that gunpower and armament were given priority over speed. Willingness to accept a top speed one or two knots slower than that of British ships enabled the Americans to construct very stout and well-armoured ships without sacrificing gunpower. Externally, U.S. battleships could be recognized by their enormous cagelike masts, described as rotary hyberloids by their admirers and as waste paper baskets by their detractors. These masts, which supported the gunnery control platforms, were undoubtedly resistant to shellfire, but their vibration and stability characteristics were not very impressive. The Russian navy, which also had these masts, soon replaced them. But it was

not until 1918, when a gale bent the mast of U.S.S. *Michigan* right down to the deck, that the U.S. Navy began to acknowledge doubts about this construction.

The eleven battleships, of which the *New York* and the *Texas* were the first, mounted 14-inch guns, compared to the 13·5-inch of contemporary British battleships. The first five had ten of these weapons, but in the later ships the use of triple instead of twin turrets enabled twelve guns to be carried. Secondary armament was provided by 5-inch guns along the sides in casemates. Although other navies had successfully adopted turbine propulsion, the *New York* and the *Texas* had the old type of reciprocating engines. Technical problems with turbines, and differences of opinion with the turbine-builders, prevented the U.S. Navy finally adopting turbines until the later *Pennsylvania* and *Arizona* were built. Nevertheless, the *Texas* and *New York* reached their designed twenty-one knots on trials.

The *Texas* served with Britain's Grand Fleet for the final year of the First World War and then, from 1925 to 1927, was modernized in the light of wartime experience. Underwater protection was improved by the fitting of bulges outside, and an additional torpedo bulkhead inside. Beneath the engine-room a triple bottom replaced the previous double bottom. Horizontal protection was enhanced, the upper of the two 3-inch decks being replaced by a 4-inch deck. Oil-fired replaced coal-fired boilers and because fewer boilers were required it was possible to replace the two funnels with one, slightly bigger. The 'waste paper baskets' were replaced by tripod masts. A catapult and three aircraft were added. In 1938 the *Texas* and her sister the *New York* were the first U.S. battleships to be fitted with radar.

In mid-1941, when the U.S.A. was still technically at peace with the world, the *Texas* was pursued for sixteen hours by a U-boat which was unable to reach a good attacking position. Some German officers regarded this as a suitable 'warning' to the Americans, but

Every inch a 'battlewagon' : U.S.S. Texas
at sea in 1944

Hitler insisted that no more similar 'warnings' should be administered; he wanted no trouble with the U.S.A. at that stage of the war. As it happened, the *Texas* had not noticed the U-boat.

For much of the war the *Texas*, the *New York* and the even older *Arkansas* formed the 3rd Battleship Division. From 1942 to 1944 the *Texas* operated in the Atlantic, mainly as a convoy escort but with occasional spells of shore bombardment. In November 1942 she supported the landings in North Africa, but her gunnery was not very successful. The local army commander did not relish the idea of 14-inch shells landing anywhere near his own troops and therefore called up cruisers rather than battleships for assistance. When the *Texas* was allowed to fire at an ammunition dump no results were obtained, partly because the dump was on a reverse slope and partly because the fifty-nine 14-inch shells which were fired were of an armour-piercing rather than high explosive type. But later, at almost ten miles range, the *Texas* fired 214 shells to break up a column of troop-carrying trucks.

In the Normandy landings the *Texas* again had little success. In company with other ships she bombarded a battery of German 6-inch guns which was hindering operations off Omaha Beach. But the Germans had quietly removed these guns to a site about a mile away, a fact which was discovered not by the ships but by

advancing U.S. troops. Later, in the advance on Cherbourg, the *Arkansas* and the *Texas* were detailed to quell a German battery of four 11-inch guns. These, protected by armour plate and concrete, could outrange the larger but older naval guns. Although the *Arkansas* fired fifty-eight 12-inch and the *Texas* 206 14-inch shells only one shell, from the *Texas*, obtained a direct hit. Thus only one of the German guns had been put out of action when the battleships, damaged, had to retire. The *Texas* had to go to Plymouth for repairs. Luckily several of the German shells failed to explode; one officer subsequently discovered an 11-inch shell reposing by his bunk. Better results were achieved in August, when the *Texas* and other battleships supported landings in southern France. Off St Tropez they silenced the German defences so effectively that the troop landings were achieved almost without casualties.

In September 1944 the 3rd Battleship Division was transferred to the Pacific, and was soon once more engaged in bombardment, the main work of British and U.S. battleships in the final years of the war. The *Texas* spent three weeks supporting the operations against Iwo Jima, and then for three months served in the Okinawa operations. Against this island she fired no fewer than 2,000 14-inch shells, after which her gun barrels must have been worn to the point of uselessness. This was her last operation. She spent eighteen months in reserve and from 1948 became a floating museum in a specially prepared berth near Houston in Texas.

THE KONGO

The *Kongo* was the oldest Japanese battleship participating in the Second World War although, thanks to successive rebuildings, she was by no means the least useful. In fact she and her three sisters led a far more active life than the other battleships because their high speed suited them for operations which would have been risky for slower ships.

The *Kongo* is also noteworthy because she was the last Japanese battleship built in Britain. When the modern Japanese navy was created in the late nineteenth century it was with the assistance of British naval officers, and British-built ships were almost exclusively used. Japanese officers trained in British naval colleges, and others spent long periods attached to the dockyards building their navy's new ships. Some of the links between the two navies lasted until 1941, and even after that it was possible to recognize British origins in many of the routines and customs of the Japanese navy.

At about the time of the Russo-Japanese War of 1904–5 Japan started to build its own battleships, having already acquired some experience in building cruisers. However, the sudden advance in ship size following Britain's *Dreadnought* in 1906 upset the Japanese plans. They had been trying to build battleships which would be bigger and better than those of other nations, and armoured cruisers which would be faster and more heavily gunned, but Britain's *Dreadnought* and Britain's battlecruisers made the Japanese designs obsolete. So to catch up with British naval technology it was decided to order a super-battlecruiser from a British yard, at the same time using British help in constructing three similar ships in Japanese yards. The *Kongo* was the lead ship of this quartet, which was confidently and justifiably expected to be world-beating. In 1910 Vickers received the order. Competition had been vigorous and, according to evidence presented to a Japanese

court in 1914, about £100,000 had been passed in bribes to Japanese officials, several of whom were sent to gaol.

Fourteen-inch guns were chosen. Thanks to friendly relations with the British navy, Japan discovered that Britain was soon to introduce the 13·5-inch gun, and immediately decided to go one better. The ship was to resemble the latest British battlecruisers of the *Lion* class, but would carry the 14-inch gun in place of the 13·5-inch. Vickers was at the time building one of the *Lions* and this ship (the *Princess Royal*) was taken as a model for most of the details. However, in several other respects the *Kongo* was superior to contemporary British battlecruisers. In particular, the situation of the third turret abaft the sternmost funnel was an improvement on the *Lion*, which had this turret inconveniently placed between the funnels. The subsequent British *Tiger* followed the Japanese example. That British builders should design for foreign customers ships superior to those being built for the Royal Navy was by no means unprecedented: British design requirements were decided by bureaucratic procedures in the Admiralty, and were not always as demanding as the requirements of foreign navies, which could, if dissatisfied, place their orders in non-British yards.

The *Kongo* was completed in 1913, the first capital ship to mount 14-inch guns. The Japanese would subsequently place great stress on outdoing other navies in gun calibre: in 1920 the *Nagato* would be the first battleship to carry 16-inch guns, and in 1941 the *Yamato* would appear with monster 18-inch guns. But this superiority in calibre never brought the Japanese any advantage, partly because their battleships were rarely in action against other battleships and partly because their gunnery was never as good as they thought.

The *Kongo*'s three sisters *Hiei*, *Haruna*, and *Kirishima* were completed by Japanese yards in 1914 and 1915. With their heavy guns and high speed (twenty-seven knots) they made an outstanding quartet. So outstanding, in fact,

The Kongo *after her final reconstruction.*
The unusual spacing of her after turrets
attracted much comment when she first appeared

that the British tried to lease two of them in 1917. But the Japanese government politely explained that these ships were so dear to the hearts of the Japanese people that, despite the celebrated Anglo-Japanese Alliance, there could be no question of them operating with the British navy.

Between the wars these ships were twice rebuilt. After the first modernization, which gave them increased deck armour and anti-torpedo bulges, their speed was somewhat reduced and they were reclassified as battleships. Then, in the thirties, they were widened and lengthened and fitted with more powerful engines. The latter gave them a speed of thirty knots, which made them once more very superior ships. Their protection, however, was not quite up to the standards of the battleships being built by the various naval powers in the late thirties. In their final form armour accounted for thirty per cent of the total weight, compared to the corresponding forty per cent of the new U.S.S. *Washington*. Also, with their eight 5-inch anti-aircraft guns the *Kongo* class ships were weak in comparison with the British *King George V* and the U.S.S. *Washington*, which carried sixteen and twenty anti-aircraft guns, although no weaker than British and U.S. battleships of similar age.

The *Kongo*, accompanied by her sister *Haruna*, provided the battleship cover for the Japanese attack on Malaya and the Dutch East Indies. The two battleships were intended to counter H.M.S. *Prince of Wales* and H.M.S. *Repulse*, which were of similar speed, but the latter pair was destroyed by land-based Japanese naval aircraft before it could be brought to action by surface ships. In April 1942 the four *Kongo* class battleships accompanied a powerful aircraft carrier force into the Indian Ocean. Although they were unable to find the main British forces, the Japanese carrier aircraft raided ports in Ceylon and sank the small British aircraft carrier *Hermes* and two cruisers. After this the British Eastern Fleet retired westwards as far as it could go, basing itself in Kenya for the next couple of years. In this way the Japanese made safe the sea supply route to their armies advancing in Burma. What would have happened to British shipping routes to India if the Japanese had prolonged this incursion can be imagined, but luckily for the British the

Top : The Kongo's *sister* Haruna *as originally built in 1915*
Bottom : The Kongo *in dry dock. The form of her anti-torpedo bulges can be discerned beneath the timberwork*

Japanese command decided, after the U.S. carrier attack on Tokyo (see p. 74), that its aircraft carriers were needed closer to the homeland.

The *Kongo*'s next big operation was to provide cover for the disastrous Japanese attack on Midway in June 1942. After this she went south and in October 1942 took part in the Guadalcanal operations. Japanese and U.S. troops were battling for this key island, and the Americans had the advantage of possessing Henderson Airfield, which gave them mastery in the air. The only way the Japanese could counter this was repeatedly to send in cruisers and battleships to bombard the airfield under cover of darkness. Only the *Kongo* class battleships had sufficient speed to enable the approach and retirement to be carried out in the short time available. The *Kongo* and *Haruna* made a successful raid of this series in October 1942, firing almost a thousand 14-inch shells at the airfield. But their sister ship *Hiei* was less successful on a later occasion. This ship met American cruisers and a chance 8-inch shell penetrated the weakly armoured steering compartment. With her rudder jammed in an extreme position, the *Hiei* could not escape, and after being assailed the following day by U.S. planes was finally scuttled. The next night the *Kirishima*, on the same duty, fell victim to the 16-inch guns of U.S.S. *Washington*, whose shells easily penetrated her armour.

In accordance with the Japanese tradition of closing the stable door after the horse has bolted, the *Kongo* and the *Haruna* were immediately provided with increased protection in the form of a thick layer of concrete around their steering compartments. The extra weight of this necessitated the removal of six of the fourteen secondary 6-inch guns.

In October 1944 the *Kongo* and the *Haruna* were with Kurita's force at the Battle for Leyte Gulf. When the order was given for a chase of the U.S. escort carriers their high speed enabled them to outpace the other ships and it is possible that it was the *Kongo*'s guns which sank the U.S. carrier *Gambier Bay* in this action. The *Kongo* was almost undamaged when she returned to the Japanese base in Borneo afterwards. However, Borneo soon became unsafe, and the *Haruna* and the *Kongo* were ordered back to Japan in November 1944.

The two battleships and their escort had already passed Formosa when they were spotted at night by the U.S. submarine *Sealion*. The latter's first radar contact had been mistaken for a land reflection and was not taken seriously until it was seen to be moving nearer. The *Sealion* then made a surface attack, firing nine torpedoes at 3,000 yards without being noticed. But the Japanese ships seemed to be unharmed and continued northwards at eighteen knots. The submarine pursued them desperately and managed to take up a position for a second attack. But before this could take place the *Kongo* slowed down, stopped, and then blew up. Apparently the *Sealion*'s torpedoes, which had seemed to miss their target, had sunk a destroyer and damaged the *Kongo*. What had gone on aboard the battleship after the hit is obscure; that she should suffer a magazine explosion two hours after the torpedo struck does raise the question of why the magazines were not flooded in time.

This question, like so many others which arise in sea warfare, has never been satisfactorily answered, but poor shipboard organization may well have been involved. The Second World War certainly showed that the Japanese were not such great seamen as they believed. Moreover, in strategy, tactics and operations the basic ingredients in Japanese attitudes were wishful thinking and medieval conceptions of correct military behaviour. Like the convoy system, damage control was 'defensive', not quite dignified, and had received insufficient attention in training. It is known, for example, that the aircraft carrier *Taiho* was lost because of this defect. Like the *Kongo*, she was struck by a torpedo which at first seemed to have caused little damage. The blast had spilled aviation fuel, and to disperse the resulting inflammable vapour all the ship's ventilators were opened. The result was that the gases were spread to all parts of the ship, which became virtually a floating bomb. When the inevitable happened the sides were blown out by an awesome explosion and the flight deck was thrown up to form 'something like a mountain range'. Quite possibly something similar took place in the *Kongo*.

THE AIRCRAFT
CARRIER

It was the Japanese who first sank a warship by air attack. This happened as early as September 1914, when an aircraft belonging to the Japanese navy dropped shells on a German minelayer off China and sank her. Later the same year the British Royal Naval Air Service made a seaplane raid on the German port of Cuxhaven. In the course of the First World War both Britain and Germany used aircraft, not very successfully, to reconnoitre for their fleets, and it was realized that, just as on land, air observation was invaluable for directing gunfire onto the targets. Moreover, by the end of the war the British had evolved practical aircraft carriers. Although seaborne aircraft were then still regarded simply as tools for reconnaissance and gunnery observation, by the beginning of the Second World War the aircraft carrier rivalled the battleship as the prime fighting unit.

When the First World War ended, the Royal Navy's aircraft-carrying ships comprised a number of seaplane carriers, whose disadvantage was that they had to stop in order to transfer their aircraft between deck and sea, and two ships which could launch and land conventional wheeled aircraft. One of these ships was the *Furious*, a battlecruiser fitted with a flying deck. Landing on this ship was somewhat perilous because of the hot gases streaming from her central funnel, but the other aircraft carrier, the *Argus*, had an all-over flight deck and no funnels (the boiler exhaust was ducted and released aft). The existence of these two ships, together with the building of two others (the *Eagle* and the *Hermes*) emphasized the leading role of Britain in this new form of warfare. In addition, the Royal Navy's experience included the sinking as early as 1915 of an enemy freighter with a torpedo dropped by a low-flying seaplane, and a successful bombing raid by aircraft from the *Furious*. When in the twenties two more battlecruisers were converted to aircraft carriers (the *Courageous* and the *Glorious*) and the *Furious* was rebuilt to eliminate her troublesome funnel, it seemed clear that the Royal Navy was destined to remain pre-eminent. But by 1930, despite her numerical superiority in carriers, Britain was already being overtaken: naval air power was not simply a question of aircraft carriers but also of aircraft and training, and in both of these the U.S.A. and Japan were pushing ahead.

Japanese aircraft carrier development owed much to a British mission which visited Japan in 1921–3. Consisting of officers who had wartime air experience (several of whom later took posts in the Japanese aviation industry), this mission shared its experience with its host country and trained the first Japanese naval airmen. Japan's initial aircraft carrier *Hosho*, like the *Hermes* designed as an aircraft carrier right from the start, flew off its first aircraft in 1922. In the late twenties two larger carriers (the *Akagi* and the *Kaga*), converted from battlecruisers, entered service. The Japanese, while watching closely the experience of Britain and the U.S.A., were not slow to work out their own methods, and soon showed great interest in torpedo-launching aircraft. Whereas British and

German airforce dogma subordinated the torpedo to the bomb,
both the Americans and the Japanese preferred the torpedo
because it was 'better to let water in through the bottom than air
out through the top'.

The U.S.A. had pioneered the launching of aircraft from
stationary ships in 1911, but it was not until 1922 that she completed her first aircraft carrier, a converted tanker. In 1927 she
commissioned two converted battlecruisers as carriers, the
33,000-ton *Lexington* and *Saratoga*. The Navy Department was
not fond of this pair, believing that it would have been better to
have built several small carriers rather than a few large ones, and its
next carrier (the *Ranger*) was a small ship of 14,500 tons. Although
it is probably true that the British continued to lead in technical
innovation, it was not long before the Americans achieved supremacy in the numbers and quality of aircraft, and in the techniques of handling them. One indication of the latter was the
larger number of aircraft which were stowed and handled by U.S.
carriers. For example, the small *Ranger* could if necessary handle
seventy-five aircraft, twice as many as the much larger British
Courageous.

The development of British naval aviation was hampered by the
struggle between the R.A.F. and the Admiralty for control of the
naval air services. The almost total transfer of control to the R.A.F.,
imposed in 1918, was progressively relaxed, but until 1937 the
Admiralty was partly dependent on the R.A.F. for aircrew, and
wholly dependent on the R.A.F. for aircraft. As the R.A.F. was
obsessed at this time with the joys of strategic bombing, it had
little interest in naval needs, with the result that throughout the
thirties and forties British naval aircraft were inferior to those of
other countries. All the same, in the building and design of carriers
it seemed that Britain in the thirties was destined to remain the

59

After the *Ark Royal*, H.M.S. *Illustrious* was the most celebrated of the British carriers. Here she is shown beneath the 6-in. guns of a British cruiser

leading power. The *Ark Royal* (laid down in 1934) was designed to accommodate sixty aircraft on a displacement of 22,000 tons. In the later thirties six more carriers were ordered. Although in size and appearance these resembled the *Ark Royal* they were actually of a novel design. Essentially an aircraft carrier consists of a flight deck, beneath which is the hangar deck where the aircraft are stored and serviced; below these two decks comes the main hull, which resembles that of a conventional warship. Hitherto, carriers had been provided only with light waterline armour and an armoured deck beneath the hangar floor. It was accepted that they were, by their nature, vulnerable ships. However, in their six new vessels the British did armour the flight decks so as to limit the damage which a bomb or plunging shell might cause. Moreover, these vessels had not only 3-inch armour on the flight and hangar decks, but also armoured hangar sides and ends. The hangar thereby formed a protective box for the inflammable aircraft. However, the extra weight meant that fewer aircraft could be carried: the first of the new carriers, H.M.S. *Illustrious*, at first accommodated only thirty-six planes.

The value of armoured flight decks was proved in the war, especially in the Mediterranean where the *Illustrious* and her sisters withstood bomb hits which would have destroyed other carriers. In 1945, too, British carriers were not badly damaged by Japanese suicide pilots who crashed into their flight decks, whereas U.S. carriers, with their easily penetrated flight decks, tended to catch fire easily when struck by bombs or suicide planes. On the other hand, the limited number of aircraft accommodated by British carriers was a severe handicap. Carriers were expected

CARRIER STRENGTH, SEPTEMBER 1939

Carrier Strength, September 1939

	Completed	Building
Britain	7	6
France	1	1*
U.S.A.	5	2
Germany		1*
Japan	6	2

*never completed

THE WORLD'S CARRIERS, BUILT OR BUILDING, SEPTEMBER 1939

Name	Year completed or converted	Displacement (tons)	Aircraft (approx.)	Main gun armament	Speed (knots)
Britain					
Furious	1918	22,500	33	12 4·5-in D.P.	30
Argus	1918	14,000	20	6 4-in	20
Hermes	1923	10,850	15	6 5·5-in	24
Eagle	1924	22,790	30	9 6-in	24
Courageous	1925	22,500	35	16 4·7-in	31
Glorious	1927	22,500	35	16 4·7-in	31
Ark Royal	1938	22,000	60	16 4·5-in D.P.	30
Illustrious	1940	25,500	54	16 4·5-in D.P.	31
Formidable	1940	25,500	54	16 4·5-in D.P.	31
Victorious	1941	25,500	54	16 4·5-in D.P.	31
Indomitable	1941	25,500	65	16 4·5-in D.P.	31
Indefatigable	1944	26,000	72	16 4·5-in D.P.	32
Implacable	1944	26,000	72	16 4·5-in D.P.	32
France					
Bearn	1927	21,800	40	8 6·1-in	21
Joffre	—	35,000	60	8 5·1-in	32
U.S.A.					
Saratoga	1927	33,000	120	8 8-in	33
Lexington	1927	33,000	120	8 8-in	33
Ranger	1934	14,000	75	8 5-in D.P.	29
Yorktown	1937	20,000	80	8 5-in D.P.	34
Enterprise	1938	20,000	80	8 5-in D.P.	34
Wasp	1940	14,700	84	8 5-in D.P.	30
Hornet	1941	19,800	90	8 5-in D.P.	33
Germany					
Graf Zeppelin	—	23,200	40	16 5·9 in	34
Japan					
Hosho	1922	7,500	20	4 5·5-in	25
Akagi	1927	36,500	90	6 8-in	31
Kaga	1928	38,200	90	10 8-in	28
Ryujo	1933	10,600	48	8 5-in	29
Soryu	1937	18,800	71	12 5-in D.P.	34
Hiryu	1939	20,000	73	12 5-in D.P.	34
Shokaku	1941	25,675	84	16 5-in D.P.	34
Zuikaku	1941	25,675	84	16 5-in D.P.	34

to provide bombers, fighters, torpedo and reconnaissance aircraft, and a ship which could fly off only thirty-six aircraft provided only small numbers of each category. Later in the war the *Illustrious* was able to operate up to sixty aircraft, after the adoption of the American practice of stowing a proportion on deck, and two of her sisters were designed from the start to handle seventy-two planes. Nevertheless, in the most massive British carrier operation of the war, the attack on Sumatran oil refineries in 1945, three modern British carriers could only muster 126 aircraft between them.

In the two years separating the outbreak of the war in Europe from the war in the Pacific, both the U.S.A. and Japan hurriedly strove to increase their carrier forces. The U.S. Navy laid down the first of its *Essex* type carriers. These, destined to play a key role in the Pacific war, were of 27,000 tons and could carry 110 aircraft. In December 1941 there were five of this class under construction, and another nineteen were built later. Simultaneously, the U.S.A. in cooperation with Britain was converting merchant ships into escort carriers (see p. 145). Also, soon after the Pacific war began, nine cruisers under construction were completed as fast light aircraft carriers. These, the *Independence* class, were of 10,000 tons and accommodated up to forty-five aircraft. Japan's effort to develop its carrier forces emphasized conversions from liners, oilers and tenders. In all, seventeen fleet carriers were built or converted by Japan during the war. Among them were the 29,300-ton *Taiho*, the 24,000-ton sisters *Hiyo* and *Junyo*, the 11,000-ton *Zuiho* and *Shoho*, and the *Shinano*, a 65,000-ton ex-battleship which despite its size carried only forty-seven aircraft. Britain built a handful of 13,000-ton aircraft carriers, but these arrived too late to take an effective part in the war.

As for the aircraft designed to operate from the carriers, the Japanese navy was probably the best equipped. The Zero was the world's best naval fighter, even though it was of somewhat fragile construction, and the dive bomber (derived from a German design) was also good. The U.S. Navy had some designs which could match these, but in December 1941 they were only just coming into service. In that month, the month of Pearl Harbor, Japan had 429 aircraft embarked in carriers and the U.S.A. 521, but the American total was divided between the Atlantic and the Pacific. As for Britain's Fleet Air Arm, this still depended on the Swordfish, a sturdy biplane of rather poor performance. Used for reconnaissance, torpedo-dropping, and bombing, this plane fell an easy victim to hostile fighters; its speed was so low that against headwinds it sometimes had difficulty catching up with its carrier. But by 1945 new designs, many of them American, were in use.

Britain's first wartime application of carrier power was ill-conceived and disastrous: using carrier aircraft to hunt U-boats resulted only in the loss by torpedo of the *Courageous*. In 1940, carrier aircraft were crucial in the Norwegian campaign, often being the only air support available for the troops ashore. The first major warship ever to be sunk by air attack was the German

H.M.S. *Formidable*, preparing to launch her *Swordfish* aircraft

cruiser *Königsberg*, which fell victim to the Fleet Air Arm's bombs at Bergen. But the Royal Navy lost the *Glorious* in this campaign: on her way home from Norway she was caught by the *Scharnhorst* and sunk, taking with her almost all her crew, including many much-needed R.A.F. and naval airmen. When the war spread to the Mediterranean in 1940, Britain's remaining carriers were really too few to supply the navy's needs. The narrow waters of the central Mediterranean were perilous for large ships, as they were covered by hostile land-based aircraft as well as by the Italian navy, strong both in surface ships and submarines. Yet despite the high risks the Royal Navy had to pass convoys to beleaguered Malta and to the armies in North Africa, and at the same time deny as far as possible the use of these strategic waters to the enemy. Convoys to Malta, attacks on enemy supply ships and transports plying to North Africa, and the evacuation of Crete, caused the Royal Navy its heaviest losses of the war. Nevertheless, several successful actions were undertaken, although two aircraft carriers were sunk and one badly damaged. The Italian navy was hit hard, and deterred from straying too far from its bases. In 1940, there was the spectacular attack on the Italian naval base of Taranto, which may be regarded as the Fleet Air Arm's finest hour. Just twenty-one Swordfish aircraft took part, flown off at night from the *Illustrious* when about 180 miles from the target. Achieving surprise, they torpedoed three of Italy's six battleships. Although two of these were later repaired, the action transformed the balance of naval power in the Mediterranean at a very critical time. In 1941 successful torpedo attacks by Swordfish aircraft from the *Formidable* slowed down an Italian squadron, enabling British battleships to catch up and win the Battle of Cape Matapan.

63

The impressive results of the attacks on Taranto, the first defeat of a battlefleet by naval aircraft, together with nostalgic memories of Japan's own surprise attack on the Russians at Port Arthur in 1904, were the inspiration of the Japanese navy's attack on the American Pacific Fleet at Pearl Harbor in December 1941. Six Japanese carriers, covered by two battleships, launched 353 aircraft against the unsuspecting Americans. Unfortunately for the Japanese, who fully realized the crucial importance of carriers in a vast battlefield like the Pacific, the U.S. carriers were not in port at the time. Bombs and torpedoes destroyed or damaged the eight U.S. battleships, but this was not enough. Having lost its battleships, the U.S. Pacific Fleet was forced to practise a strategy based on its aircraft carriers, which was in fact the best strategy.

The first true carrier battle, fought by aircraft against carriers without the ships ever coming into contact, was the Battle of the Coral Sea in May 1942. The Japanese, still on the offensive, were attempting to land in the Solomons and in New Guinea. They sent one force, including the newly converted carrier *Shoho*, to cover the New Guinea landing, and a stronger force with the carriers *Shokaku* and *Zuikaku* towards the Solomons. To meet these two thrusts the Americans could send only the carriers *Lexington* and *Yorktown*. Bad visibility, misidentification of ships, and mistakes in radio transmissions plagued both sides, and it was the successes and failures of reconnaissance which largely determined the result of the action. Luck and judgement helped U.S. planes to locate the *Shoho*, which was sent to the bottom with thirteen bomb and seven torpedo hits. The main Japanese and U.S. forces, despite intense reconnaissance, long failed to locate each other. But after dark returning Japanese aircraft attempted to land on the U.S. carriers, believing them to be their own. From this disconcerting mistake both commanders deduced that the opposing carrier forces must be close, and both despatched scout planes at daybreak. Both almost simultaneously located the other, and both immediately launched bomber and torpedo strikes. The result was that the *Lexington* was sunk and the *Shokaku* badly damaged. Although technically this was a Japanese victory, in effect the Americans won, because the *Shokaku* and *Zuikaku*, having lost many precious aircrews, were unable to take part in the crucial Battle of Midway.

The Battle of Midway marked the turning point of the Pacific war. In the Coral Sea the Japanese had been stopped in their tracks, but at Midway their losses of carriers and trained aircrews put them on the defensive for the rest of the war. The Japanese plan was to devote six carriers and supporting heavy ships to an attack on Midway Island, with the aim of luring the U.S. fleet into an air, surface and submarine trap. But, thanks to timely intelligence reports, the U.S. carriers advanced unseen and unexpected towards the attackers. Aircraft from the three U.S. carriers (the *Enterprise*, *Hornet* and *Yorktown*) caught the Japanese with their planes down. While the Japanese were successfully defending themselves against the low-flying U.S. torpedo bombers, high-flying dive bombers swooped down and scored fatal hits on three carriers (the *Kaga*, *Akagi* and *Soryu*). Later in the battle a fourth Japanese carrier (the *Hiryu*) went down, but U.S.S. *Yorktown* was finally located and damaged by the Japanese, being finished off by a Japanese submarine. This was the first big defeat suffered by the Japanese nation since the sixteenth century, and the facts about it were not revealed to the Japanese public.

After Midway, and with new ships joining the fleet, the Pacific was more or less dominated by U.S. task forces consisting of carrier groups supported by fast battleships and cruisers. Carriers provided cover over both sea and land, allowing the expulsion of Japanese garrisons from one island after another. Two further naval battles in 1944, in the Philippine Sea and near Leyte Gulf, put an end to Japanese sea power. U.S. carriers played the major role in both these battles, which opened the way for the final advance towards Japan itself.

Below: The Japanese carrier *Shokaku*, photographed shortly before leaving for the Pearl Harbor operations in 1941

Bottom: The Essex-class carriers joined the U.S. fleet during the war. Here the *Yorktown* (the second carrier of that name) is shown in the Pacific in late 1944

H.M.S. ARK ROYAL

H.M.S. *Ark Royal* was perhaps the most celebrated aircraft carrier of the Second World War and certainly the only ship to derive much of its glamour from enemy propaganda. 'Lord Haw-Haw', the broadcaster of German radio propaganda intended for British listeners, on a number of occasions announced that the *Ark Royal* had just been sunk, and that the British Admiralty refused to admit the loss. 'Where is the *Ark Royal*?' he repeatedly asked his amused listeners. It is believed that the German pilot, whose genuinely daring attack on the ship had been the cause of the first 'sinking', later committed suicide; despite his own modest claims, he had been decorated and celebrated for destroying the ship and was therefore put in an insufferable position when the propagandists sank the *Ark Royal* on a second occasion. But, propaganda apart, the *Ark Royal* led a very active wartime life.

Completed in 1938, the *Ark Royal* was of about the same size as the earlier *Courageous* and *Glorious* and incorporated much of the experience gained with those two ships. She was of 22,000 tons, 800 feet long and 94 feet wide. She carried about sixty aircraft and could steam at thirty knots, stowing enough fuel to cruise 12,000 miles. She carried a crew of about 1,600 men. Her anti-aircraft armament was stronger than previous carriers, despite the difficulty of arranging gun positions which would not unduly hinder flight deck operations. She carried sixteen 4·5-inch dual-purpose weapons and a large number of smaller anti-aircraft guns. Since British carriers were expected to operate in waters dominated by enemy land-based aircraft and since they would accommodate only a few fighters (and these of inferior design), emphasis on a strong anti-aircraft defence seemed justified.

The *Ark Royal* began the war inauspiciously. Allocated to anti-submarine patrols, she was lucky to escape the torpedo of a lurking U-boat. Three of her aircraft which attacked another U-boat were signally unsuccessful. Their bombs missed, and the blast of the explosions downed two of them, while the third flew off after making vain machine gun attacks. The U-boat then surfaced to pick up the crews of the ditched aircraft and went home. But, in that same first month of the war, the *Ark Royal*'s aircraft redeemed themselves in the North Sea by shooting down a German flying boat; this was Britain's first victory against the Luftwaffe. The latter retaliated by sending a bomber force against the ship. In preparation for this the *Ark Royal*'s aircraft, including her fighters, were stowed safely away and their fuel tanks emptied. Reliance was placed on anti-aircraft gunfire from the carrier and her consorts. The gunfire did in fact deter four of the five attackers, but the fifth pressed on and scored a near miss. This was the first 'sinking' of the *Ark Royal* claimed by the Germans.

Later the carrier formed part of a detachment unsuccessfully hunting for German raiders in the Atlantic. But her reconnaissance aircraft brought about the interception of several German blockade-runners. In 1940 her aircraft took part in the Norway campaign and almost immediately afterwards the carrier was sent south as a founder-member of the celebrated Force H at Gibraltar. The first task of Force H, formed just as France was surrendering, was to neutralize the French warships at Oran. As the French admiral refused all the choices presented to him, designed to ensure that his ships could never fall into German hands, Force H opened fire. Most of the French ships were put out of action by gunfire, but the *Ark Royal*'s aircraft failed in their endeavours to stop the escape of the battleship *Strasbourg* to France. Later in 1940 the *Ark Royal* participated in the unsuccessful attempt to land troops (and General de Gaulle) at Dakar. The *Ark Royal*'s aircraft tried but failed to damage the battleship *Richelieu*, and just failed to warn in time the battleship H.M.S. *Resolution* that a French submarine was attacking. After the bedraggled Allied force had retired, towing the *Resolution*, the *Ark Royal* returned to Gibraltar.

In the following months the *Ark Royal*

H.M.S. Ark Royal *in 1938. The continuation of the side plating up to the flight deck, a characteristic of British carriers, can be clearly seen*

operated in the Mediterranean and Atlantic. Her aircrews were not as well trained as they should have been, and although their reconnaissance and fighter activities were invaluable, their rare attacks on enemy warships were unsuccessful. At the Battle of Cape Spartivento, in which an attack by Italian battleships and cruisers on a Malta convoy was frustrated, the *Ark Royal*'s aircraft made two torpedo attacks. But the slow Swordfish biplanes, moving only about forty m.p.h. faster than their target, were easily out-manoeuvred. Despite heavy attacks by land-based aircraft the *Ark Royal* retired to Gibraltar; by this time there was no longer any reluctance to defend the ship with her own fighters. Early in 1941 her aircraft tried unsuccessfully to torpedo a dam in Sardinia, but had more luck when they bombed Pisa and Leghorn. They also directed the gunfire of ships bombarding Genoa. These attacks on the Italian mainland, as intended, had a valuable effect on Italian morale, not very high in any case.

In March 1941 the *Ark Royal* and the *Renown* were searching for the *Scharnhorst* and the *Gneisenau*, at large in the Atlantic. One of the carrier's aircraft did sight the German battleships, but a broken screw in its radio prevented an immediate report; the resulting delay permitted the Germans to reach Brest safely. But in May the *Ark Royal* had better success. Again with the *Renown*, she was directed into the Atlantic to search for the *Bismarck*. Heavy seas and fifty-m.p.h. winds made flying-off unprecedentedly perilous. Getting the aircraft lined up required teams of men hanging grimly onto the machines to prevent them being blown overboard. The take-offs had to be timed so that each aircraft would leave the pitching flight deck just as the ship's bows were on the rise. Even so, several planes skimmed the waves before climbing into the low cloud. On this occasion the antiquated Swordfish was ideal, being more manoeuvrable and having a shorter take-off than more modern monoplanes. Soon the fugitive *Bismarck* was found and shadowed by Swordfish. Fourteen torpedo-carrying Swordfish were then despatched: a successful air attack seemed the only way to slow down the German battleship sufficiently to enable the British battleships to catch up with her. But the Swordfish, hampered by poor visibility, by mistake attacked the cruiser H.M.S. *Sheffield*. Fortunately the magnetic detonators of the torpedoes were faulty and this, together with frenzied manoeuvring by the cruiser, averted

67

*A destroyer removes the crew of the sinking
Ark Royal in 1941*

a disaster. After the Swordfish returned to the
carrier a second attack of fifteen aircraft was
launched. This time the torpedoes used contact
detonators and two of them not only hit the
Bismarck but exploded satisfactorily. The battleship's steering was damaged, ensuring her
destruction by gunfire a few hours later. The
Ark Royal was approached by German bombers
while in the act of recovering her aircraft, but
anti-aircraft gunfire from the accompanying
battlecruiser *Renown* kept them at a safe
distance, a reminder that aircraft carriers needed
the support of heavy ships.

Back in the Mediterranean, the *Ark Royal*
continued to cover the Malta convoys, and
sometimes flew off to the island new deliveries
of R.A.F. fighters. It was in tasks such as these

that she really justified her existence. Her aircraft may not have shot down many enemies but
they prevented coordinated bombing attacks
by breaking up attacking formations, and they
kept shadowing aircraft away from British
operations. Conducting fleet operations within
range of enemy airfields would have been very
dangerous without carriers. It was while on
these routine duties that the *Ark Royal* was
hit by a single torpedo from a German submarine. This killed only one man, but it put
the ship's telephones out of action. Damage
control measures were thereby delayed – and
damage control in aircraft carriers was at that
time very much an unexplored science in any
case. So, despite a long struggle to tow her home,
the '*Ark*' eventually sank just twenty-five miles
from Gibraltar. Everybody, including a ginger
tom cat, was safely taken off.

'Lord Haw-Haw' soon announced that the
Ark Royal had been sunk, but not everyone
believed him.

U.S.S. ENTERPRISE

The U.S. government, much sooner than the British, accepted that in an economic depression the state should undertake not less, but more, public investment. The Roosevelt government, faced with the unemployment of the thirties, therefore established the Public Works Administration. One of the projects undertaken by the Administration was the building of two aircraft carriers, the *Enterprise* and the *Yorktown*. In 1942 this pair of ships, built to beat unemployment, played a crucial part in beating Japan.

Approved in the 1934 building programme, the *Enterprise* and the *Yorktown* were commissioned in 1938 and 1937 respectively; the former had been delayed when defects were discovered which necessitated the replacing of hundreds of boiler and bearing components. Of 20,000 tons, these ships brought U.S. carrier tonnage almost up to the treaty limit, so the next carrier (the *Wasp*) was of less than 15,000 tons. However, during the late thirties the treaty restrictions lost their effect, and one week after the commissioning of the *Enterprise* a half-sister was started. This, U.S.S. *Hornet*, was almost indistinguishable from the *Yorktown* and *Enterprise*.

The design of this pair influenced the later carriers of the *Essex* class. At the time, 20,000 tons was regarded by many naval aviators as the minimum size which would enable a carrier to be self-contained, able to defend itself as well as to attack and to scout. Maximum aircraft capacity was eighty, although in practice fewer were carried; in 1941 the *Enterprise* carried eighteen fighters, thirty-six dive-bombers, and eighteen torpedo bombers. Eight 5-inch dual purpose guns were mounted, as well as thirty-two automatic anti-aircraft guns. There was a 4-inch belt of armour at the waterline, and the hangar deck was armoured with 3-inch plate. The flight deck was covered with 6-inch hardwood planking; not until later in the war would U.S. carriers be built with armoured flight decks. Unlike British carriers, in which the hull side plating was curved outwards up to the flight deck, the *Enterprise* and the *Yorktown* had flat sides, with wide openings along the hangar deck. These openings could be closed by sliding doors in rough weather, but when open they increased ventilation and illumination, thereby improving the working conditions of the mechanics. These openings also made possible the catapult-launching of aircraft directly from the hangar deck, although in service this facility was not used; with three high-speed elevators linking the flight and hangar decks, the rapid launching of aircraft was assured in any case. Another facility which was provided but not used was the arrangement of arrestor wires both forward and aft. This made it possible to land planes from two directions but, again, caused handling and organization problems. For heavily-loaded planes, and for no-wind conditions, two flight-deck catapults were provided.

In this design the U.S. Navy finally opted for a tall funnel and island structure on the starboard side. Like the British, but unlike the Japanese, the Americans had decided that this was the best way to solve the problem of boiler fumes. Exhaust from vents in the side or stern allowed a clear flight deck but created worse turbulence.

When Japan attacked Pearl Harbor the U.S.A. had three aircraft carriers in the Pacific (the *Lexington, Saratoga* and *Enterprise*). The *Enterprise* was on her way back from delivering fighters to the Marines on Wake Island and, but for heavy seas, would have been in or near Pearl Harbor at the time of the attack. When she was about 200 miles from Pearl Harbor she sent off her bombers to the airfield which they habitually used when the ship was in port. On approaching land, the pilots of these aircraft noticed anti-aircraft gunfire, but thought it was practice. Then they were pounced on by Zero fighters, and realized that this was no practice. But for seven of them this realization came too late. Some of those that did land safely took part in the subsequent search for the retiring Japanese aircraft carriers, and four

Manoeuvring violently, the Enterprise *tries unsuccessfully to evade Japanese bombs*
Inset : The Enterprise *operating torpedo aircraft in 1943*

were shot down by 'friendly' anti-aircraft guns when they returned to base. Meanwhile the *Enterprise* had received a radio message: 'Air raid Pearl Harbor. This is no drill.' As the bombers which she used as scouts had already gone, the *Enterprise* was not able to take a very effective part in the search for the Japanese. Those ships and planes which did participate raised a number of false alarms but never found the Japanese. A radio message from one aircraft, 'No carriers in sight', was transmitted as 'Two carriers in sight', whereupon the *Enterprise* despatched her torpedo aircraft to this

non-existent target. Another aircraft spotted the cruiser U.S.S. *Portland* and reported the sighting of an enemy aircraft carrier disguised as an American cruiser. The *Enterprise's* fighters, which had escorted the abortive torpedo strike, had insufficient fuel to return to the carrier and therefore went to an airfield, where half of them were shot down by American anti-aircraft artillery. Meanwhile the torpedo aircraft had to land in the dark, still loaded. This unpractised manoeuvre was successfully executed, although one torpedo broke loose as its aircraft touched down on the *Enterprise's* flight deck. Luckily a crew member, mounted astride the slithering torpedo, brought it to a halt before it could cause any damage.

The *Enterprise* entered Pearl Harbor the day following the Japanese attack. Smoke was still rising from the half-sunken battleships, and rescue parties were cutting through the hulls to extricate sailors trapped in their compartments. Fires were smouldering ashore, and the water was covered with spilled fuel oil. The carrier remained only eight hours, and then put to sea. The search was now on for Japanese submarines which had taken part in the attack but had not yet left the area. Two torpedoes were seen to pass close to the *Enterprise*, one passing only about twenty yards from her stern. However, despite the American lack of caution, the Japanese did not succeed in torpedoing any of the U.S. carriers. Instead, they lost one of their big 2,000-ton submarines which was dive-bombed by one of the *Enterprise*'s planes, and finished off by another. This submarine was the first major warship lost by the Japanese in the war.

A week after Pearl Harbor, the *Enterprise* (or the 'Big E', as she was called) was deployed in support of the half-hearted attempt to relieve Wake Island. Then, in January, she was used to escort convoys to Samoa. In this work she was joined by her sister the *Yorktown*, which with three battleships had been hastily transferred from the Atlantic. The two carriers also raided atolls in the Marshall Islands, where the Japanese had built air bases. During one of these raids the 'Big E' was attacked by Japanese bombers, one of which dived on the ship in an apparent suicide exploit. But a crew member leapt into a plane parked on deck and with its rear machine gun beat off the attacker. The air raids on the atolls were the first American attacks on Japanese territory.

In April 1942 the *Enterprise* participated in a much bigger raid on Japanese territory, on Tokyo itself. The carrier *Hornet* was carrying large bombers on her flight deck and could not handle fighter and reconnaissance aircraft. It was to provide such aircraft that the *Enterprise* was part of the attacking force. Her scouts spotted Japanese patrol boats, stationed much further from Japan than had been expected. Surprise was now unlikely, and Admiral Halsey ordered the bombers to take off when the force was about 650 miles from Japan, instead of the intended 500 miles. But as the Japanese did not know that the raiders would be long-range army

planes, they calculated that the carriers would steam for several more hours before launching the planes. Surprise, after all, was achieved because of this miscalculation, and the effect was enhanced by the practice air raid alarm which was just finishing as the raiders approached Tokyo. It was not until the bombs had been dropped that the local defenders realised that this was a real attack.

After the Tokyo raid the *Enterprise* and the *Hornet* ferried fighters to New Caledonia. Having missed the Battle of the Coral Sea by one day, the *Enterprise* was ordered back to Pearl Harbor in anticipation of the Japanese attack on Midway Island. On 28 May the *Enterprise* and *Hornet* left Pearl Harbor and took on their planes at sea. The first plane to land on the *Enterprise* skidded over the side, but the others landed safely. Two days later the *Yorktown* also left Pearl Harbor; because of damage received in the Battle of the Coral Sea she needed three months of repairs, but was patched up by 1,400 shipyard workers in less than two days. By June 2 the three carriers were about 325 miles north of Midway, unknown to the advancing Japanese. The *Enterprise* and *Hornet*, with attendant cruisers and destroyers, formed one task force, while the *Yorktown* and her escort formed another. The Japanese carriers launched air strikes against the island on June 4, and at the same time the U.S. carriers launched their own attacks, even though the position of the Japanese ships was not precisely known. The *Enterprise* launched her aircraft when she was about 200 miles from the target. Her torpedo bombers, like those from the other carriers, did not have full fighter protection; consequently only four of the fourteen returned, and no hits were scored. But while the Japanese were successfully defending themselves against low-level torpedo planes, thirty-two high-flying dive bombers from the *Enterprise*, taking advantage of scattered clouds, moved into position unnoticed. When they began their dives the Japanese carriers were just beginning to launch refuelled and rearmed planes. The bombs therefore fell on highly inflammable targets and the *Akagi* and *Kaga* were soon crippled by fires and explosions. Then the *Yorktown*'s bombers attacked the *Soryu*, and Japanese naval supremacy in the Pacific was at an end. Admiral Yamamoto, commanding the Japanese forces far in the rear, realized the catastrophe which had befallen his attempt to lure the American carriers into a trap. Nevertheless, he issued a message to his men saying that the U.S. fleet was shattered and in full retreat.

Because the *Enterprise*'s aircraft had been launched beyond their nominal range of action, many came down in the sea. Radio silence, preventing the direction of returning aircraft which had lost their way, made matters worse. But the 'Big E' compensated for some of her ditched aircraft by accepting fifteen dive bombers from the *Yorktown*, which had been damaged and would later be sunk.

Later that day the *Enterprise* sent twenty-four of her own and the *Yorktown*'s dive bombers to attack the fourth and last carrier of the Japanese force. This, the *Hiryu*, was sunk. When she went down she took with her Admiral Yamaguchi, who had decided to lash himself to the sinking ship. Yamaguchi, a former student of Princeton University, was probably the most intelligent of the Japanese admirals and, if he had lived, would almost certainly have succeeded Yamamoto as commander in chief. The following day, *Enterprise* and *Yorktown* aircraft sank the fleeing Japanese cruiser *Mikuma*.

Two months later the 'Big E' was supporting the invasion of the Solomon Islands. At the Battle of the East Solomons, dive bombers from the Japanese *Shokaku* and *Zuikaku* were located almost a hundred miles away as they approached. At the time, the fighter direction officers of the *Enterprise* controlled fifty-three airborne fighters from the *Enterprise* and *Saratoga*. But those fifty-three fighters had garrulous pilots, whose radio chatter prevented the instructions from the *Enterprise* being received. So although many of the attackers were shot down, about two dozen were able to dive-bomb the *Enterprise*, scoring three hits and starting fires. After an hour the fires were extinguished and the carrier was taking on her planes. But then her rudder jammed. Water had entered her steering engine compartment, short-circuiting the motor. Smoke had already overcome the local engineers, and it was half an hour before rescuers could reach the compartment and start the stand-by

motor. During that half-hour, with the carrier unable to steer, the second wave of Japanese aircraft should have attacked. But thanks to a navigational error on the part of the Japanese, this attack never took place.

In late October 1942 the *Enterprise* was damaged by Japanese carrier aircraft at the Battle of Santa Cruz. Repairs were interrupted by an urgent call for carrier support off Guadalcanal. With repair crews still on board, and with her forward elevator still out of action, the carrier steamed towards the island. She sent some of her aircraft to operate from Henderson airfield, and these discovered and helped to destroy the battleship *Hiei*, damaged by U.S. cruisers the previous night. On the same day the *Enterprise*'s aircraft took the major part in sinking the Japanese cruiser *Kinugasa*, and others attacked transports. One of the *Enterprise* pilots, shot down by anti-aircraft fire, spent 73 hours in the water before swimming to an island. In the afternoon the carrier was attacked by Japanese aircraft. At the time her few remaining fighters were not airborne, but once again she was lucky; a rain squall hid her long enough to frustrate the Japanese attack.

In May 1943 the *Enterprise* went for ten weeks of much-needed repairs. During this period she was replaced in the south-west Pacific by H.M.S. *Victorious*.

Later in the war the 'Big E' took part in the Battle of the Philippine Sea, where one of her scouts first spotted Japan's 1st Mobile Fleet. Her attack planes, launched at targets beyond their nominal radius of action, had difficulty in returning. Many went down in the sea and others crashed on landing. Some pilots, out of fuel, landed against orders and crashed into other aircraft in the darkness. One plane landed with its firing key still open, and its machine guns blazed away as it touched down.

A few months later the *Enterprise* took part in the Battle for Leyte Gulf. Her aircraft were the first to locate Nishimura's force approaching from the south, and later they helped to sink the battleship *Musashi*. By this time many new carriers had joined the U.S. Navy, which meant that the *Enterprise* was not the vital basic element she had been in 1942. But she took part in all the subsequent major amphibious opera-

A pre-war view of the Enterprise's *sister,*
U.S.S. Yorktown, *showing the open hangar*
deck favoured by U.S. designers

tions against Japanese-held islands, specializing in night work. During the Gilbert Islands operations in late 1943 the U.S. Navy for the first time used carrier fighters at night. This happened after the *Enterprise* had been troubled by Japanese night bombers. She sent up an Avenger torpedo bomber which, unlike her fighters, had radar. This bomber was followed into the air by two fighters, which followed it towards the Japanese bomber force that had been picked up on the radar. The Japanese were taken by surprise, but in the resulting melée one of the U.S. fighters, flown by a famous ace, disappeared, apparently shot down in error by the Avenger. So the experiment was not a complete success, and moreover it was claimed that the presence in the air of friendly aircraft made the task of the anti-aircraft gunners almost impossible at night. Nevertheless, in February 1944 the 'Big E' launched the first U.S. carrier night attack, when twelve radar-equipped Avengers were catapulted to raid Japanese shipping at Truk. By this time the ship had eighteen fighters and twenty-seven Avengers with radar and, apart from the newer and smaller *Independence*, was the only carrier suited for night work. There was still some opposition to night operations. The deck crews complained

that landing and launching was far more difficult at night. Also, an erroneous impression was formed of the night fighter crews, who were thought to be not quite pulling their weight. Because they slept during the day, when Japanese attacks were most frequent, and worked unseen at night, this impression was natural, but unfortunate. However, night operations continued and from mid-1944 the *Independence* and *Enterprise* operated together as a specialised task force.

In the Okinawa operation the *Enterprise* received a not uncommon type of damage: anti-aircraft shells from nearby ships burst over her flight deck, killing seven men and starting ammunition and aviation fuel fires. After brief repairs she rejoined the fray, only to be damaged by two Japanese suicide planes. A third suicide plane's bomb penetrated deep inside the ship before exploding, putting the *Enterprise* out of action for the rest of the war.

The *Enterprise* was repaired in time to take part in 'Operation Magic Carpet', the carrying home of U.S. servicemen. In this role she made two transatlantic trips. She was decommissioned in 1956, and scrapped in 1958 after attempts to preserve her as a relic had failed. Certainly she deserved to be preserved, for she had taken part in more major actions than any other U.S. ship. Of the twenty-two principal Pacific actions, the 'Big E' had missed only the Battle of the Coral Sea and the final raids on Japan.

U.S.S. HORNET

U.S.S. *Hornet* was completed in late 1941, just before the U.S.A. entered the war. Very similar to the preceding *Yorktown* and *Enterprise*, she was of 20,000 tons and her overall length was 810 feet and width 114 feet. She carried 4-inch armour on the waterline and the deck (floor) of her hangar was of 3-inch plate to protect, among other things, the 187,000 gallons of aviation fuel stored below. Despite the weight of armour she could reach thirty-three knots. In wartime she carried a crew of almost 3,000 men. Her maximum aircraft capacity was 100 but in fact seventy-two was the preferred number, divided equally between fighters, reconnaissance bombers, bombers and torpedo planes. In common with other U.S. aircraft carriers, she had a relatively weak gun armament, finding space only for eight 5-inch dual-purpose guns and thirty-nine rapid-firing smaller weapons.

Her first exploit occurred in April 1942, lightening the gloomy period of successive American defeats. This was the celebrated raid on Tokyo, undertaken mainly for its effect on American and Japanese morale and on world opinion. As naval bombers were too small for this mission, sixteen twin-engined army bombers were used. These were of the B-25 type, the largest bomber which could be flown off the *Hornet*'s deck. Escorted by the *Enterprise* and four cruisers, the *Hornet*, despite heavy seas, successfully launched the bombers when about 650 miles from Japan. Tokyo and other cities were bombed and the aircraft, as planned, attempted to reach Chinese airfields. Only one bomber succeeded in landing safely in China, although of the eighty aircrew only seven lost their lives, three of them being executed by the Japanese, allegedly as punishment for dropping bombs on civilian targets.

In June 1942 the *Hornet* and the *Enterprise* formed the nucleus of one of the two U.S. task forces which defeated the Japanese at Midway. She took into this battle twenty-seven fighters, thirty-seven reconnaissance dive bombers and fifteen torpedo planes; she emerged from it with fifteen fighters and twenty-seven bombers. Her torpedo squadron was entirely shot down; only one man survived, and he only because he could float concealed beneath a seat cushion until the Japanese disappeared. None of the U.S. torpedo bombers scored hits, but their efforts were not in vain. The gunfire and evasive manoeuvring which they caused hampered the launching of aircraft from the Japanese flight decks, and while they were drawing Japanese eyes towards sea level the U.S. dive bombers got into position for their subsequent devastating attack.

For the remainder of her short life the *Hornet*

The first U.S. bomber leaves U.S.S. Hornet *to make the 1942 raid on Tokyo*

was in the South Pacific, assisting U.S. land forces in the reconquest of the Solomon Islands. Her aircraft attacked targets on sea and on land, and at times she ferried aircraft to newly conquered air bases. In September 1942 her consort, the aircraft carrier *Wasp*, was torpedoed and sunk by a Japanese submarine; the *Wasp's* aircraft which were already in the air landed on the *Hornet*, and for a time the latter was the only serviceable U.S. carrier in the Pacific. But in October, soon after being joined by the partly repaired *Enterprise*, the *Hornet* was sunk by Japanese carrier aircraft off the Santa Cruz islands. Her aircraft, with those from the *Enterprise*, were flown off to attack a Japanese force consisting of carriers and battleships, but on the way to their target they passed in mid-air a Japanese striking force directed against their own carriers. The Japanese bombers concentrated on the *Hornet* and, because the latter's available fighters had been launched too late to reach a good height, the attacks were successful. Five bombs, as well as two torpedoes, struck the carrier. When her own aircraft returned after helping seriously to damage a cruiser and the carrier *Shokaku*, they found their ship crippled and ablaze and had to land on the *Enterprise*. The latter was soon attacked but, thanks to a heavy anti-aircraft barrage from the new battleship *South Dakota*, was not badly damaged. However, the *Enterprise* group was withdrawn to avoid further Japanese attacks, leaving the *Hornet* exposed as a target for the Japanese pilots. She was abandoned after another torpedo and two bombs had struck her.

But, as with other carrier casualties, the *Hornet* took a long time to sink. Carriers did not behave as other ships, they seemed more buoyant and able to list at terrifying angles without capsizing; it is likely that several British, American and Japanese carrier losses could have been avoided if damage control had been better studied. In the *Hornet's* case, U.S. destroyers tried to sink her with torpedoes and several hundred shells, but failed. It was not until several hours later, after Japanese destroyers had hit the derelict hulk with four large torpedoes, that she finally sank. She had lived only fifty-three weeks, but few ships of the Second World War played a more decisive role than that of the *Hornet*.

U.S.S. LEXINGTON

Of all the naval powers, the U.S.A. had the most battleships and battlecruisers under construction when the Washington Naval Treaty was signed in 1922. Most of these had to be abandoned but two, the battlecruisers *Saratoga* and *Lexington*, were redesigned as aircraft carriers. At 33,000 tons, they were long regarded as the world's largest aircraft carriers and in the interwar years enabled the U.S. Navy to gain experience and superiority in the handling of carrier aircraft. But as the U.S.A. was restricted by the Washington Treaty to a total aircraft carrier tonnage of 135,000, the existence of these two large ships meant that the number of carriers in the U.S. Navy would be rather limited. In fact, the subsequent *Ranger* and *Wasp* were small ships precisely because of the need to keep total tonnage below 135,000.

With her huge slab of a funnel (actually enclosing four separate rectangular smokestacks) the *Lexington* was not a handsome ship. But she was certainly an effective ship. She could handle eighty aircraft as a normal complement, and was capable of carrying a total of 120. Her eight 8-inch guns were not very useful, but imitated the practice of other countries at the time. These cruiser-size guns prevented the installation of a more powerful anti-aircraft armament although it was found possible to install twelve 5-inch guns. Early in the war the 8-inch guns were removed: since the *Lexington* and *Saratoga* were expected to operate with cruiser or battleship cover they did not need these weapons. The ship was 888 feet long, and the 180,000-horsepower engines could move her huge bulk at thirty-four knots. These were the most powerful engines installed in a warship, and on trial they actually developed 210,000 shaft horsepower. The bow was of bulbous form, slightly decreasing water resistance and providing better support for the forward part of the ship.

When the Japanese attacked Pearl Harbor, the *Lexington* was delivering aircraft to island garrisons, while her sister the *Saratoga* was visiting the U.S.A. Soon after returning to Pearl Harbor the *Lexington* participated in the abortive attempt to relieve Wake Island, an operation of which the details were long concealed from the American public. The first Japanese landing on this American island outpost had been repelled by the Marines, but the attempt was renewed from 12 December. Admiral Kimmel planned a naval strike against the Japanese invasion force, but this was not pressed home. Three carriers (the *Lexington*, *Saratoga*, and *Enterprise*) were used, with escorting cruisers and destroyers. An initial delay occurred when it was discovered that the *Lexington* could not fuel at sea because of the rough weather. Two days after leaving Pearl Harbor the *Lexington*'s scout aircraft reported the sighting of a Japanese carrier, but the thirty-six aircraft sent to attack it discovered that it was not a carrier but an abandoned U.S. ammunition barge. Then a practice firing revealed that most of the anti-aircraft ammunition of the cruisers and destroyers was defective. The *Saratoga* group stopped to refuel the destroyers just when decisive action was needed, and in the middle of the operation Kimmel, who was held responsible for the Pearl Harbor disaster, was replaced by Nimitz. Nimitz, however, was in Washington. With all these troubles, the new and temporary commander on the spot decided to abandon the project. The Japanese conquered Wake Island, but in retrospect it seems that they would have suffered a defeat if the American attack had gone forward as planned.

In February 1942 the *Lexington* with her four cruisers and ten destroyers temporarily joined the ANZAC forces to make a surprise raid on Japanese troops and ships at Rabaul in New Guinea. For the *Lexington* this was a risky venture because the scene of operations was 3,000 miles from Pearl Harbor, with its repair and fuelling facilities. Moreover, the only available charts for the area were based on the work of eighteenth-century explorers. The force was soon sighted by a Japanese flying boat, and air attacks developed. There were air battles above the *Lexington*, many of whose crew went on

deck to cheer, until their admiral reminded them that this was not a football match. The *Lexington*'s fighters shot down several Japanese aircraft, and the carrier was not damaged. However, because surprise was lost the attack on Rabaul was abandoned.

The *Lexington*'s first and only major engagement was in the Battle of the Coral Sea. At this time she carried seventy-one aircraft (twenty-three Wildcat fighters, thirty-six Dauntless dive bombers, twelve Devastator torpedo bombers) and most of these participated in the ninety-three-plane attack on the Japanese carrier *Shoho*. This, the first attack by U.S. planes on a carrier, resulted in the sinking of the target. In a later phase of this battle the *Lexington*'s torpedo bombers failed to locate the carrier *Shokaku*, but four of her scouting bombers added to the damage inflicted on that carrier by planes from U.S.S. *Yorktown*. Meanwhile the Japanese carrier planes had been attacking the two U.S. carriers. The latter were steaming together inside a circle of cruisers and destroyers. This escorting circle raised a strong anti-aircraft barrage, but this was not enough to offset the small number of U.S. fighters in the air. Japanese torpedo planes attacked the *Lexington* simultaneously on both sides. About eleven

U.S.S. Lexington : *a pre-war photograph*

torpedoes were dropped, at a range of about half a mile, and two of them hit the carrier. With a turning circle not far short of 2,000 yards the *Lexington*'s evading action could not be agile and, moreover, the evasions of the carriers disorganized the circle of escorting ships, leaving more gaps in the anti-aircraft defence. This gave the Japanese dive bombers their chance, and they scored two hits. At this climax of the battle the *Lexington*'s siren jammed at full blast, making life even more difficult for those on board. Nevertheless, the *Lexington* continued to take on her planes and it seemed that everything was under control. But, just after the damage control officer had reported that the ship was safe, there was a loud explosion, followed by others. Apparently a generator spark had ignited fumes from spilt aviation fuel. The fire spread explosively; many men were burned unnecessarily by flash because they were clothed too scantily. But the crew was safely evacuated by a destroyer; even the captain's dog was saved. The *Lexington* was slow to sink, and in the end five torpedoes were needed to send her to the bottom.

77

THE AKAGI

Like the U.S.A., Japan had a great naval expansion programme under way at the time the Washington Treaty was signed. Like the U.S.A. she decided to convert two uncompleted battle-cruisers into aircraft carriers. These were the *Akagi* and *Amagi*, but the latter was so badly damaged by an earthquake that the conversion was abandoned and the battleship *Kaga* substituted. It is for this reason that the *Akagi* and *Kaga*, which formed the backbone of Japanese naval aviation between the wars, and which operated together until both were lost on the same day, were not true sister-ships.

As originally completed, the *Akagi* was a flush deck carrier with one true flight deck and two additional flying-off decks. The latter were extensions of the upper and lower hangars, whose decks were carried forward into the open air, creating a stepped-up silhouette. However, in 1937–8 the *Akagi* was modernized. Her flying-off decks were eliminated and her flight deck extended forward. This deck sloped downwards fore and aft so that planes would land uphill and take off downhill. An island superstructure, containing the command position and aircraft control equipment, was added, but this did not include the funnel as in the carriers of other countries. Instead, in an effort to carry exhaust well away from landing planes, a wide funnel projected outwards and downwards from the ship's side. As reconstructed, the carrier displaced 36,500 tons, had an overall length of 855 feet and width of 103 feet. She could carry ninety-one aircraft (of which twenty-five were spare) and had a complement of 1,340 men. She carried six 8-inch guns in casemates along the side and had an anti-aircraft defence of twelve 4·7-inch and twenty-eight 25-mm guns. With her 5,770 tons of oil she could cruise for about 8,000 miles.

The *Akagi* was the flagship of Vice-Admiral Nagumo during her short wartime career. With the five other carriers of the Japanese main striking force, she led the surprise attack on Pearl Harbor. Subsequently she was with the striking force in the South Pacific, supporting the Japanese advance against New Guinea and Java. On 19 February 1942 her aircraft participated in the raid on Darwin which sank twelve ships, devastated the docks and prevented their use by the Allies for many months. Local inhabitants took refuge in the countryside and thirty years later Australians were still arguing about what actually happened that day. In April, finally to eliminate the British Eastern Fleet and to prepare the way for land operations in Burma and against India, these carriers with their supporting ships entered the Indian Ocean. The Royal Navy's old battleships kept out of their way (finally finding refuge in East Africa) but during operations against Ceylon the Japanese carrier planes found and sank the British carrier *Hermes* and the cruisers *Dorsetshire* and *Cornwall*. However, by this time the Japanese had lost so many planes and trained

aircrew that a return to Japan became advisable. Shortage of aircrew would plague the Japanese navy for the rest of the war, and was aggravated by the Japanese predilection for glorious self-sacrifice – massive sacrifice of infantrymen might have won the Russo-Japanese War, but the massive sacrifice of highly trained pilots in this war could only be catastrophic.

Meanwhile the U.S. carrier raid on Tokyo had persuaded the Japanese to keep their carriers nearer home. To destroy the troublesome U.S. carriers the Midway operation was planned, and in this the *Akagi* was again Nagumo's flagship. This battle shattered the Japanese striking force. The *Akagi* was preparing her planes for a second strike against Midway Island when the news came that American carriers were in the vicinity. Nagumo ordered a strike to be prepared against these, but while his aircraft were

crowded on the flight and hangar decks the first U.S. planes arrived. Dive bombers from U.S.S. *Enterprise* scored three hits, one of which fell among the planes on the flight deck while another detonated torpedoes in the hangar deck. After this there was little hope for the blazing *Akagi*, but Nagumo, a hot-tempered man, refused to leave his bridge. When eventually he was dragged away the ladders had disappeared. So the Admiral and his staff officers had to scamper down a rope. After this they hopped around on the searing deck amid exploding ammunition, burning their hands and feet before they were rescued. The Sacred Portrait of the Emperor, as usual in such cases, fared better: it was carefully wrapped and entrusted to a destroyer. According to one account, the captain of the *Akagi*, eager to uphold the stirring traditions of the Japanese navy, tied himself to the ship's anchor, but was subsequently persuaded to end this exhibition and rejoin his men. Finally, helped on her way by Japanese torpedoes, the *Akagi* went down.

The Akagi *in 1941*

THE ZUIKAKU

The *Zuikaku* and her sister the *Shokaku* were both ordered in 1937 and their completion in 1941 was one of the factors determining the date of the Japanese attack on Pearl Harbor. The design was based on the preceding *Hiryu*, but they were larger ships (25,700 tons, 845 feet long). They could carry seventy-two aircraft, plus twelve spare, and with their three elevators and two catapults could quickly get these into the air. Five thousand tons of oil gave them a range of almost 10,000 miles. They were protected from air attack by an armoured hangar deck of almost seven inches and by sixteen 5-inch and thirty-six 25-mm guns. During the war they were fitted with thirty-four additional 25-mm weapons. These two sisters operated together, usually as part of the striking force. The latter, at the time of Pearl Harbor, consisted of six carriers, two battleships, two heavy cruisers, and a light cruiser leading sixteen destroyers.

However, at the Battle of the Coral Sea the *Zuikaku* and *Shokaku* were detached. In this battle the *Zuikaku* escaped damage because a rain squall hid her just as the American planes attacked. But she lost most of her aircraft and had to return to Japan to form new squadrons. Thus she missed the Battle of Midway, where her presence and that of the *Shokaku* might well have turned the balance. In the later Battle of the Eastern Solomons, her planes, with those from the *Shokaku*, damaged the *Enterprise*, whereas the U.S. attacking force was unable to locate the two Japanese carriers.

In June 1944, hoping to win a big naval victory which would transform the strategic situation, the Japanese planned an attack on American Task Force 58 (15 carriers, 7 battleships, 21 cruisers, 69 destroyers, 891 carrier aircraft and 65 shipborne seaplanes). For this the Japanese force (the 'Mobile Fleet') comprised 9 carriers, including the *Zuikaku*, 5 battleships, 13 cruisers, 28 destroyers, 430 carrier aircraft and 43 seaplanes. The disparity in numbers was to be compensated by directing the Japanese carrier planes to land on Japanese-held islands after making their attack on the U.S. force; this in effect would enable the Japanese carriers to launch their planes while still out of range of the American aircraft. However, this plan was not realized, largely because preliminary American air attacks rendered the Japanese air bases useless. Moreover, the Japanese aircrews were inexperienced and only partly trained. The result was that the Japanese attacking planes were shot down in huge numbers. Meanwhile the *Shokaku* was torpedoed by a U.S. submarine and the com-

The Zuikaku *on the eve of war (left) and (above) taking violent action to avoid American bombs during the Battle of the Philippine Sea*

manding admiral was forced to leave this doomed carrier for the safety of the *Zuikaku*. This was more or less the end of the Battle of the Philippine Sea. The Japanese retired, having lost most of their aircraft and aircrews. The *Zuikaku* had been damaged by air attack.

So short were the Japanese of planes and crews that in the final big naval battle, the Battle for Leyte Gulf, the *Zuikaku* and five other carriers were used simply as bait. They were to lure the U.S. battleships and fleet carriers away from the beaches of Leyte Gulf, where American troops had landed in the Philippines campaign. Two Japanese battleship groups would then converge on the uncovered U.S. transports and sink them. The decoy succeeded; the U.S. fast battleships and carriers moved northwards and their air attacks sank the *Zuikaku* and three light carriers. But this sacrifice was in vain, for the other two Japanese striking forces were turned back with heavy losses by old battleships, torpedo craft and escort carriers.

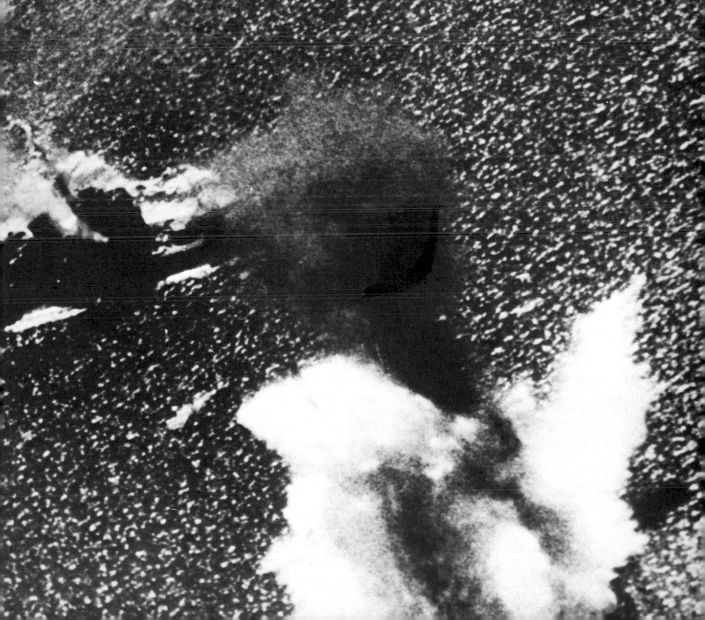

THE CRUISER

For Britain, which at the end of the First World War was still the greatest naval power, the cruiser was perhaps the most appreciated type of warship. When serving with the Grand Fleet, cruisers had been entrusted with scouting, with strengthening the destroyer flotillas, and with combating enemy cruisers. Elsewhere the British cruiser had had an equally important, genuinely 'cruising', role, patrolling the trade routes in wartime and 'showing the flag' in peacetime in all parts of the world touched by British seaborne trade. This latter kind of work demanded somewhat different qualities from those needed for fleet cruisers; in particular, long range and good habitability were needed. It became accepted that Britain could never without great risk reduce her cruiser strength to below seventy units (she ended the First World War with 120).

That other island sea power, Japan, had somewhat different requirements, and Japanese policy more than British policy shaped the development of the world's cruiser fleets in the interwar period. Whereas Britain's cruiser requirement reflected her need to defend those worldwide assets which she had already won, Japan's was directed more to acquiring such assets. For the Japanese, whose strategic concepts had always been rather primitive, this meant that Japanese warships had simply to be bigger and better than those of the powers most likely to oppose her. Since the Washington Treaty prevented this bigger and better policy being applied to battleships, it was adopted most markedly for cruisers. Eventually, Japanese designs prompted first the U.S.A., and then Britain, to build cruisers bigger than they might otherwise have been. For the Americans, large cruisers would in any case have been preferable, because of the long ranges at which a Pacific war would be fought, but it is doubtful whether the U.S. Navy would have equipped its cruisers with such heavy gun armaments had it not felt the need to compete with Japan. While it is true that both Japan and the U.S.A. appreciated the cruiser as a scout, as a cheap substitute for the battleship, and as an escort against both armoured ships and destroyers, the main reason each of these two countries built large cruisers was because each was trying to outdo the other.

For the three continental naval powers, things were simpler. Germany was limited until 1935 by the Versailles Treaty and could only build a few ships of moderate size. France had little to fear from the German navy and could therefore concentrate on matching Italy. Italy only needed to match France. (For this reason the French and Italian cruisers were similar; both tended to sacrifice protection for very high speeds, the result being a series of ships which were not only well-suited for fleeing from other cruisers, but had little safe alternative.)

The Washington Treaty did not prevent the powers from building large cruisers, but since it classified ships of over 10,000 tons as battleships, and severely limited that category, its signatories could not build cruisers above that tonnage without sacrificing some of the tonnage allowed them for battleships. At the same time

a maximum gun calibre was determined for cruisers. Britain, which was building a handful of cruisers with 7·5-inch guns, successfully proposed that the maximum calibre should be 8 inches. This was a notable example of a short-term advantage being won at a heavy long-term price, for every naval power at once began to build 10,000-ton cruisers with 8-inch guns, whereas what Britain needed was smaller ships with 6-inch guns. Britain could not afford to build numerous big cruisers; her money would have been better spent on a larger number of smaller ships.

Japan and Italy were the first to lay down the new 'Treaty' cruisers, in 1923. Their designs were very different. The *Trento* and *Trieste*, in the Italian tradition, were very fast (35-knot) ships carrying eight 8-inch guns but rather lightly built. The Japanese pair, *Furutaka* and *Kako*, carried only six 8-inch guns, were designed for thirty-three knots, and were quite well armoured. The Italians went on to build five more heavy cruisers, the final four of which were more sturdy and less fast. The Japanese built two more cruisers with six 8-inch guns and then produced the four *Myoko* class ships. These, on an alleged displacement of less than 10,000 tons, managed to include ten 8-inch guns, extensive armour (four inches thick on the side) and engines producing a speed of almost thirty-four knots. Moreover, on the eve of the war these cruisers, like many other Japanese cruisers, were equipped with the new 24-inch long-range torpedoes. The *Myoko* class was soon followed by the four similar ships of the *Takao* class.

The U.S.A. was late starting on the construction of heavy cruisers, most of her ships in this category being completed in the early thirties. But the American designs never seemed quite to achieve the Japanese fighting qualities. This was hardly surprising, because while the American designers kept quite close to the 10,000-ton limitation the Japanese deliberately and quietly exceeded it; the

85

After temporary repairs, H.M.S. *Exeter* steams home after the River Plate engagement

Myoko type was probably about 13,000 tons, the Japanese publicly ascribing the success of this design to the weight savings achieved by welding and to the lesser living space needed by the smaller and tougher Japanese sailor. The first American cruisers (the *Pensacola* and *Salt Lake City*) had two triple and two twin 8-inch gun turrets with the heavier triple turrets being in the upper position; not surprisingly, these ships were top-heavy and subsequent designs mounted nine 8-inch guns instead of ten, and these were in just three turrets. Britain meanwhile had been building its distinctive 'County' class cruisers. These were high-sided, three-funnelled ships mounting eight 8-inch guns in four twin turrets. Because their side armour was almost non-existent and because of their big silhouette these ships were regarded as rather vulnerable, almost as white elephants. In fact they were a useful class, very stable and seaworthy, and with a long range (over 10,000 miles). During the war they were used mainly on distant patrol work and proved very suited for this. Nevertheless, they were bigger ships than Britain really needed. The two subsequent 'Cathedral' class ships (the *Exeter* and *York*) were an attempt to remedy this, being smaller, better protected, and mounting only six 8-inch guns.

Largely owing to British pressure and example, construction of large 8-inch gun cruisers died out in the thirties, the 6-inch gun cruiser coming into favour. Britain preferred the 6-inch gun because it required a somewhat smaller ship to accommodate it, and in any case its greater rapidity of fire outweighed the greater range and penetrating power of the 8-inch weapon, especially in actions at night or in bad weather. Britain then introduced three classes of light cruisers, mounting eight or six 6-inch guns, having eight 4-inch anti-aircraft guns, six or eight torpedo tubes, moderate armour (two to four inches at the side) a speed of thirty-two knots and a range of up to 12,000 miles. All three of these designs (the *Leander*, *Amphion*, and *Arethusa* classes) proved very successful during the war and showed what could be achieved on a small displacement when the exaggerated space requirements of 8-inch armaments were no longer required.

CRUISER GUNS

Calibre	Weight of shell (lbs)	Range (miles)	Claimed rate of fire (rounds per minute)
British 6-inch	105	14	8
British 5·25-inch	85	14	10
U.S. 8-inch	260	18	2
German 5·9-inch	101	13	10
Italian 8-inch	275	19	3·5
Japanese 6·1-inch	122	18	10

Cruisers at Pearl Harbor in 1943: at left are the *Salt Lake City* and *Pensacola*, with their top-heavy gun arrangement, and the *New Orleans* lies next to the jetty

In the Pacific the reversion to the traditional cruiser 6-inch calibre did not result in smaller ships, but in a new competition, with the U.S. and Japanese designers seemingly sacrificing stability and other qualities in an attempt to outdo the other in gunpower. The Japanese *Mogami* class mounted no fewer than fifteen 6·1-inch guns, and the U.S.A. replied with the well-known *Brooklyn* class, also mounting fifteen main guns but with an inferior designed speed. Once again the Japanese ships exceeded the 10,000-ton maximum, probably by about twenty-five per cent. The existence of Japanese cruisers mounting fifteen 6·1-inch guns forced the British Admiralty to construct a class of larger cruisers to match them. This was the successful and well-known *Southampton* class, mounting twelve 6-inch guns on less than 10,000 tons. From the *Southampton* class were developed the bigger but not really better *Edinburgh* and *Belfast*, and the *Colony* class. The latter, another very successful class, was like the *Southampton*, but, because Britain was hoping to persuade other countries to reduce the maximum cruiser size from 10,000 to 8,000 tons, these ships were built to the latter tonnage.

On the eve of the war there was a tendency to abandon the moderate-sized cruiser in favour of more 8-inch gun ships. Japan quietly changed the armament of its two improved *Mogami* type ships from twelve 6·1-inch to eight 8-inch guns, and then converted the preceding *Mogami*s; the five triple 6·1-inch turrets were replaced by five twin 8-inch turrets. Meanwhile the U.S.A. completed the *Wichita*, which was virtually a *Brooklyn* but with nine 8-inch guns. Britain, however did not revert to the 8-inch gun, probably wisely. In the meantime Russia had laid down some Italianate cruisers, armed with 7·1-inch guns, and these had been used as a pretext by Germany to increase its heavy cruiser strength. However, neither the German nor the Russian cruisers played a significant part in the war.

A number of powers had also begun to build light cruisers with strong anti-aircraft armaments. The British *Dido* class, completed during the war, used the new 5·25-inch dual-purpose gun and was especially useful in narrow waters where both air and surface attack might be expected. Britain was already removing the 6-inch guns of some of her oldest cruisers and replacing them with eight to ten 4-inch anti-aircraft guns. In the U.S.A. the *San Diego* class of 6,000-ton cruisers was under construction. This had a main armament of sixteen 5-inch dual-purpose guns and could steam at thirty-four knots. Italy, which had been building very fast 6-inch gun cruisers in the thirties, was introducing its 3,750-ton *Regolo* class ships, mounting eight 5·3-inch dual-purpose guns and capable, it was claimed, of no less than forty-one knots. However, by that time the Italians were so proud of the high speed of their ships that they had begun to cook the books; among other things, ships' speed trials were held on exceptionally calm days with a following tide and with the ships in lightened condition, with just enough fuel for the trials and sometimes not even carrying guns.

Right: H.M.S. *Argonaut* of
the Dido class, regarded by
many as the finest design of
British light cruiser

Below left: The *Kenya*, one of
Britain's very successful
Colony-class cruisers

Below right: The
unmistakeable shape of
Britain's County-class cruiser:
H.M.S. *Cumberland* during
the war

Bottom: The heaviest
development of the British
6-in. gun cruiser, H.M.S.
Edinburgh

CRUISER STRENGTHS AND CRUISER LOSSES

Totals at time of entry into war:

	8-inch gun ships	Ships with 6·1-inch guns or smaller	total	Completed during war	War losses
Britain	17	46	63	28	32
France	7	11	18	0	9
Netherlands	0	4	4	1	3
U.S.S.R.	5	3	8	2	2
U.S.A.	18	19	37	46	10
Germany	1	6	7	2	6
Italy	7	12	19	3	13
Japan	18	17	35	5	38

N.B. Eight-inch gun totals include two British ships with 7·5-inch and five Russian with 7·1-inch guns.

CRUISERS OF THE SECOND WORLD WAR

Ships	Years of comple-tion	Ton-nage (stan-dard)	GUNS Main	Heavy A.A.	Tor-pedo tubes	Nominal speed (knots)	Air-craft
Britain and Commonwealth							
C class (6 ships)	1917–19	4,200	5 6-in	2 3-in	8	29	0
C class (7 ships)	1917–18	4,200	—	8 4-in	0	29	0
D class (8 ships)	1918–22	4,850	6 6-in	3 4-in	12	29	0
Hawkins, Frobisher	1919–24	9,800	5 or 7 7·5-in	4 or 5 4-in	4	30	0
Effingham	1925	9,550	9 6-in	8 4-in	4	30	1
Emerald, Enterprise	1926	7,550	7 6-in	3 4-in	16	33	1
Dorsetshire, Norfolk	1930	10,000	8 8-in	8 4-in	8	32	1
Devonshire, London	1930	10,000	8 8-in	8 4-in	8	32	1
Shropshire, Sussex	1930	10,000	8 8-in	8 4-in	8	32	1
Berwick, Cornwall	1928	10,000	8 8-in	8 4-in	8	32	1
Cumberland, Kent	1928	10,000	8 8-in	8 4-in	8	32	1
Suffolk, Australia	1928	10,000	8 8-in	8 4-in	8	32	1
Canberra	1928	10,000	8 8-in	8 4-in	8	32	1
York, Exeter	1930–31	8,300	6 8-in	4 4-in	6	32	1
Leander, Achilles	1933	7,200	8 6-in	8 4-in	8	32	1
Orion, Ajax, Neptune	1934–5	7,200	8 6-in	8 4-in	8	32	1
Amphion, Phaeton	1936	7,000	8 6-in	8 4-in	8	32	1
Apollo (renamed on transfer to R.A.N. *Perth, Sydney, Hobart*)	1936	7,000	8 6-in	8 4-in	8	32	1
Arethusa, Galatea,	1935	5,200	6 6-in	8 4-in	6	32	1
Penelope, Aurora	1936–7	5,200	6 6-in	8 4-in	6	32	1
Southampton, Sheffield	1937	9,400	12 6-in	8 4-in	6	32	2
Newcastle, Birmingham	1937	9,400	12 6-in	8 4-in	6	32	2
Glasgow, Gloucester	1937–9	9,400	12 6-in	8 4-in	6	32	2
Liverpool, Manchester	1938	9,400	12 6-in	8 4-in	6	32	2

Edinburgh, Belfast	1939	10,000 12 6-in	12 4-in	6	32	2
Dido, Euryalus, Naiad	1940–1	5,600	10 5·25-in D.P.	6	33	0
Phoebe, Bonaventure	1940	5,600	10 5·25-in D.P.	6	33	0
Hermione, Cleopatra	1941–2	5,600	10 5·25-in D.P.	6	33	0
Sirus, Argonaut	1942	5,600	10 5·25-in D.P.	6	33	0
Scylla, Charybdis	1942	5,600	8 4·5-in D.P.	6	33	0
Bellona, Black Prince	1943–4	6,000	8 5·25-in D.P.	6	33	0
Diadem, Royalist	1943–4	6,000	8 5·25-in D.P.	6	33	0
Spartan	1943–4	6,000	8 5·25-in D.P.	6	33	0
Fiji, Kenya, Mauritius	1940	8,500 12 6-in	8 4-in	6	33	2
Nigeria, Trinidad	1940–2	8,500 12 6-in	8 4-in	6	33	2
Ceylon, Uganda	1943	8,500 9 6-in	10 4-in	6	33	2
Jamaica, Gambia, Bermuda	1942	8,500 12 6-in	8 4-in	6	33	2
Newfoundland	1942	8,500 9 6-in	10 4-in	6	33	2
Swiftsure, Ontario	1944–5	8,000 9 6-in	10 4-in	6	32	0
Superb	1945	8,000 9 6-in	10 4-in	6	32	0

U.S.A.

Omaha class (10 ships)	1923–5	7,050 10 or 12 6-in	8 3-in	6	35	2
Salt Lake City, Pensacola	1929–30	9,100 10 8-in	8 5-in	0	32	4
Northampton, Chester	1930	9,200 9 8-in	12 5-in	0	32	4
Louisville, Chicago	1931	9,200 9 8-in	12 5-in	0	32	4
Houston, Augusta	1930–31	9,200 9 8-in	12 5-in	0	32	4
Indianapolis, Portland	1932–3	9,900 9 8-in	12 5-in	0	32	4
Astoria, Minneapolis	1934	10,000 9 8-in	12 5-in	0	32	4
New Orleans, Quincy	1934–6	10,000 9 8-in	12 5-in	0	32	4
San Francisco	1934	10,000 9 8-in	12 5-in	0	32	4
Tuscaloosa, Vincennes	1934–7	10,000 9 8-in	12 5-in	0	32	4
Brooklyn, Philadelphia	1938	10,000 15 6-in	8 5-in	0	32	4
Savannah, Nashville	1938	10,000 15 6-in	8 5-in	0	32	4
Phoenix, Boise, Honolulu	1938–9	10,000 15 6-in	8 5-in	0	32	4
St Louis, Helena	1939	10,000 15 6-in	8 5-in	6	32	4
Wichita	1939	11,000 9 8-in	8 5-in	0	32	4
San Diego class (11 ships)	1942–6	6,000 12 or 16 5-in D.P.		8	34	0
Cleveland class (27 ships)	1942–6	10,000 12 6-in	12 5-in	0	33	3
Baltimore class (14 ships)	1943–6	13,600 9 8-in	12 5-in	0	33	4

Germany

Emden	1925	5,600 8 5·9-in	3 3·5-in	4	29	0
Karlsruhe, Köln	1930	6,650 9 5·9-in	6 3·5-in	12	32	2
Königsberg	1930	6,650 9 5·9-in	6 3·5-in	12	32	2
Leipzig	1931	6,700 9 5·9-in	6 3·5-in	12	32	2
Nürnberg	1935	7,000 9 5·9-in	8 3·5-in	12	32	2

The German cruiser *Königsberg* on exercises shortly after completion

Admiral Hipper, Blücher	1939	14–15,000	8 8-in	12 4·1-in	12	32	3
Prinz Eugen	1940	14–15,000	8 8-in	12 4·1-in	12	32	3

Japan

17 light cruisers	1919–25	3–6,000	4–7 5·5-in	1–2 3-in	4–8	32–35	0–1
Furutaka, Kako	1926	9,000	6 8-in	4 4·7-in	8	33	2
Kinugasa, Aoba	1927	9,000	6 8-in	4 4·7 in	8	33	2
Myoko, Ashigara	1929	13,400	10 8-in	8 5-in	16	33	3
Nachi, Haguro	1928–9	13,400	10 8-in	8 5-in	16	33	3
Atago, Chokai	1932	13,200	10 8-in	8 5-in	16	34	3
Maya, Takao	1932	13,200	10 8-in	8 5-in	16	34	3
Mogami, Mikuma	1935	12,500	10 8-in	8 5-in	12	34	3
Suzuya, Kumano	1937	12,500	10 8-in	8 5-in	12	34	3
Tone, Chikuma	1938–9	11,200	8 8-in	8 5-in	12	35	5
Agano, Noshiro	1942–3	7,000	6 5·9 in	4 3-in	8	35	2
Yahagi, Sakawa	1942–4	7,000	6 5·9 in	4 3-in	8	35	2
Oyodo	1943	8,200	6 5·9-in	8 3·9-in	0	36	2

Italy

Bari, Taranto	1912–15	3,200	7 or 8 5·9-in	2 or 3 3-in	0	21–27	0
Trieste, Trento	1928–9	10,000	8 8-in	12 3·9-in	8	35	2
Bolzano	1933	11,000	8 8-in	12 3·9-in	8	36	2
Fiume, Gorizia, Zara	1931	11,800	8 8-in	12 3·9-in	0	32	2
Pola	1932	11,800	8 8-in	12 3·9-in	0	32	2
Giuseppe Garibaldi	1937	9,500	10 6-in	8 3·9-in	6	35	4
Luigi di Savoia Duca degli Abruzzi	1937	9,500	10 6-in	8 3·9-in	6	35	4
Eugenio di Savoia	1936	8,500	8 6-in	6 3·9-in	4–6	37	3
Emanuele Filiberto Duca d'Aosta	1935	8,500	8 6-in	6 3·9-in	4–6	37	3
Raimondo Montecuccoli	1935	8,500	8 6-in	6 3·9-in	4–6	37	3
Muzio Attendolo	1935	8,500	8 6-in	6 3·9-in	4–6	37	3
Bartolomeo Colléoni	1932	5,300	8 6-in	6 3·9-in	4	37	2
Giovanni delle Bande Nere, Luigi Cadorna	1931–3	5,300	8 6-in	6 3·9-in	4	37	2
Alberico da Barbiano	1931	5,300	8 6-in	6 3·9-in	4	37	2
Alberto di Giussano	1931	5,300	8 6-in	6 3·9-in	4	37	2
Armando Diaz	1933	5,300	8 6-in	6 3·9-in	4	37	2
Attilio Regolo	1942	3,750	8 5·3-in D.P.		8	39	0
Pompeo Magno	1943	3,750	8 5·3-in D.P.		8	39	0
Scipione Africano	1943	3,750	8 5·3-in D.P.		8	39	0

N.B. The A.A. guns of most cruisers could also be used in surface action. The notes given below the table of Battleships of the Second World War (p. 19) apply also to this table.

Friend or foe? Anti-aircraft gunners examine approaching aircraft during a U.S. cruiser operation in the Pacific

During the war only the U.S.A. laid down new cruisers on a large scale. Because American construction periods were so short a number of these joined the fleet before the war ended. Notable among these were the *Cleveland* class, with twelve 6-inch guns, and the *Baltimore* class, mounting nine 8-inch guns and being an enlarged version of the experimental *Wichita*. Other countries gave cruiser construction a low priority, largely because of doubts whether any new ships laid down could be completed in time to take part in the war. Existing cruisers tended to be modified during the war. Many British cruisers with four main turrets had the third turret replaced by anti-aircraft guns. New and heavy radar equipment required masts to be strengthened. Automatic anti-aircraft weapons were increased. British cruisers lost their scout aircraft and catapults; it was argued that escort carriers and radar made such aircraft superfluous. However, U.S. cruisers and battleships kept their aircraft, on the grounds that the more scouting aircraft were provided by these ships, the more space there would be on the aircraft carriers for fighter and attack planes.

During the war cruisers undertook most of the tasks which their designers and the theorists had envisaged, although the priorities were rather different. Actions of cruiser against cruiser were quite rare, so the efforts which admiralties had made to ensure that their own cruisers would be a match for those of their enemies were at last shown to be irrelevant; Britain's preference for small cruisers was justified. Like battleships and destroyers, cruisers were well equipped to fight surface gun actions but less well equipped to beat off air attacks, whereas in practice they were in action against aircraft many times more often than against surface targets. The role of cruisers in amphibious operations had also been underestimated, although in this case their strong surface weapons were advantageous; whereas battleships excelled against heavy fortifications at long range, the cruisers could move in close to the beaches and destroy local defences. As scout and ocean escort the cruiser proved its worth in all theatres, but especially in northern waters. On a number of occasions, both in the Atlantic and the Arctic, German heavy ships were deterred from attacking convoys simply by the presence of one or more escorting cruisers; even if the cruiser was weaker than the raider it could shadow the latter or, if the latter attacked, could inflict sufficient damage to make the long journey home a very doubtful proposition. In the Mediterranean, and in the Pacific, cruisers accompanying convoys or belonging to task forces made an important contribution to air defence.

The first important surface action was the defeat of the 'pocket battleship' *Graf Spee* by three British cruisers in 1939. Later, in the Mediterranean campaign, cruisers played an important part in scouting and in bringing the Italian ships to battle off Matapan. At the Second Battle of Sirte three *Dido* class cruisers escorting a convoy with destroyers drove off an Italian force which included a modern battleship and cruisers. Earlier, the Australian light cruiser *Sydney* had pursued two Italian cruisers and sunk one of them before they could use their high speed to get away. Force K, consisting of *Arethusa* and *Leander* type cruisers, made several successful attacks on Italian convoys carrying vital supplies to North Africa. However, it was in the Mediterranean that the British navy suffered its heaviest cruiser losses. Air attacks during the Greece and Crete operations, and submarine and air attacks on convoys to Malta, took a steady toll. Force K was routed when it ran into a minefield near Tripoli while on a raid. Several ships were badly damaged and one, the *Neptune*, was lost with all except one of her crew after striking four mines.

It was in the Pacific war that most of the few cruiser versus cruiser actions took place. Most of these, especially in the beginning, ended in Japan's favour. The Japanese had two assets in these battles: they had their 24-inch long-range torpedo, and their crews and commanders were highly trained in night operations. The 24-inch torpedo, whose qualities took the Allied navies by surprise, could travel eleven miles at forty-nine knots, whereas the 21-inch torpedoes used by the Allies could do about three miles at forty-five knots. Japanese training in night warfare was especially effective because the Americans were very inexperienced in this field, giving their enemies many easy chances. Moreover, the American superiority in radar was largely vitiated by the initial reluctance of U.S. admirals to place much faith in this equipment. It was some time, for example, before American admirals learned that the best ship from which to direct a battle was that with the best radar.

The first major cruiser action was the Allies' defeat at the Battle of the Java Sea, in February 1942. A mixed and not very well coordinated squadron of two Dutch, one British, one Australian and one U.S. cruiser encountered a Japanese force of roughly similar strength. Using their aircraft for spotting, the Japanese guns put H.M.S. *Exeter* out of action with long-range gunfire and soon afterwards, again at long range, the two Dutch cruisers were sunk by torpedoes. The surviving Allied cruisers and destroyers retired, to be sunk later as they attempted to slip southwards between the Indonesian islands.

A series of cruiser actions was fought in the Solomon Islands operations. Soon after the Americans had landed on Guadalcanal a force of Japanese cruisers (five 8-inch and two lighter cruisers) attacked Allied heavy cruisers covering the invasion transports. The Japanese approached at night, taking advantage of poor Allied lookouts. The Allied cruisers were located off Savo Island and the Japanese cruisers' aircraft dropped parachute flares to silhouette them for the benefit of the Japanese gunners. A few minutes of heavy bombardment resulted in the sinking of one Australian and three American cruisers with trifling loss to the attackers. Two months later, at the Battle of Cape Esperance in October 1942, the Americans' revenge for the Battle of Savo Island was a relative failure. Four U.S. cruisers lay in wait for three Japanese cruisers which were approaching to bombard a U.S.

The U.S. light cruiser *Atlanta* shortly before her loss in the Guadalcanal operations

airfield. Although on this occasion it was the Japanese who were surprised, they lost only one cruiser. The next month, however, the U.S. cruisers put the battleship *Hiei* out of action. This happened when the battleship, accompanied by smaller ships, attempted a night bombardment of the same vital Henderson Airfield which had earlier been the object of Japanese attention. The U.S. cruisers had no plan of attack, nor any scouts ahead, and more or less met the Japanese head-on. The result was a night battle in which neither side quite knew what it was doing, and in which both sides frequently fired on their own ships. When the battle ended the *Hiei* was so damaged that she had to be scuttled, and the Americans had lost two new light cruisers, the *Atlanta* by gunfire and the *Juneau* by submarine. The same month the Americans tried to waylay the so-called 'Tokyo Express', a frequent fast supply service by which Japanese warships, sheltered from air attacks by darkness, tried to aid their beleaguered garrison on Guadalcanal. On this occasion, the Battle of Tassafaronga, the U.S. ambush resulted in the sinking of a mere destroyer, while Japanese torpedoes sank one American cruiser and damaged others. However, this Japanese victory, which eased the supply problem, came too late, and Guadalcanal was taken by the Americans. Later, around nearby islands, similar operations took place and the Americans had better success, especially with their destroyer attacks. But they never won cruiser victories comparable to the Japanese success at Savo Island.

95

U.S.S. INDIANAPOLIS

The U.S. Navy was a late entrant in the race to build 8-inch gun cruisers, but by September 1939 she had built more of this type than any other power (eighteen units, compared to fifteen British and fourteen Japanese). These ships played a subsidiary but important role in the war, especially in 1942 before the new U.S. battleships and cruisers appeared.

They were built in four groups, the *Indianapolis* and her sister the *Portland* comprising the third group. Although generally similar to their predecessors, these ships were regarded as a distinct improvement, being less top-heavy and with thicker (though less extensive) side armour. They carried nine 8-inch guns in what was becoming the standard U.S. Navy disposition, two triple turrets forward and one aft. They also carried the standard heavy anti-aircraft armament of eight 5-inch guns. Their designed speed was 32½ knots.

The *Indianapolis* was built at Camden, New Jersey, from 1930 to 1932. Equipped as a flagship, she offered superior accommodation and for this reason was chosen to take President Roosevelt on his South American 'good neighbor' cruise in 1936. When the war started the cruiser was based at Pearl Harbor, but she was training at sea when the Japanese struck. In early 1942 she operated with aircraft carriers around New Guinea before going for refit and then to the Aleutian Islands in the North Pacific. In the campaign to recapture those islands which had been occupied by the Japanese, the *Indianapolis* carried out a few shore bombardments in the intervals between the thick fogs of that region. Her biggest success in this area was the interception at night of a Japanese munitions ship. When challenged, the latter replied in Japanese Morse and the *Indianapolis* opened fire on her at 6,700 yards. U.S. destroyers then moved in to finish her off, but all six of their torpedoes missed or misfired. She was finally dealt with by destroyer gunfire.

During the war the *Indianapolis* had several refits, in which her automatic light anti-aircraft guns were increased, and improved fire

control directors fitted. After a refit in spring 1943 she left to become the flagship of the Fifth Fleet. In this role she participated both as a headquarters ship and as a bombardment ship in the successive invasions of Pacific islands, beginning with Tarawa and ending with Okinawa. Off the latter island she was damaged by a Japanese suicide plane. The plane was knocked into the water by anti-aircraft fire, but its pilot managed to release his bomb just before crash-

ing. This bomb penetrated the armoured deck, passed right through the ship and exploded beneath the bottom. The cruiser was saved but had to go to San Francisco for repairs.

After these repairs the *Indianapolis* received high-priority crates and passengers for transport to the Pacific island of Tinian. After the ten-day transit needed to cover the 5,000 miles, she duly delivered her cargo (which was the atomic bomb, due to be dropped on Hiroshima), and went to the Guam naval base. From there she was despatched to the Philippines.

She never arrived. Moving leisurely through waters which were supposed to be safe, she was struck by two torpedoes from the Japanese submarine I-58. She sank in twelve minutes, taking a third of her 1,200-man crew with her. Because it was not unusual for ships to be delayed, no alarm was raised for three days. It was only when a patrol aircraft happened to spot men floating in their lifejackets that a rescue effort was made. By that time only about 300 men were left to be picked up.

The Indianapolis *during her last visit to the U.S.A., in July 1945*

THE MOGAMI

Although Japanese designers did exceed the treaty limitations on warship size, they also made great efforts to reduce the weight of new ships. After all, violations could not be too obvious; it was only in the thirties, when Japan had formally withdrawn from the naval treaties, that she began to practise large-scale deception on the outside world. In the twenties, so great an effort was made to reduce weight that a number of designs were frail or unstable. This was revealed when Japanese warships steamed through a typhoon, with disastrous results. After this a number of ships were scheduled for modification. Among these were the brand new *Mogami* and her sisters. Their turrets, of which there were no fewer than five, impaired stability, while the electric welding employed to keep down the weight of their hulls had resulted in a seriously weakened structure.

The *Mogami* had been laid down in 1931, the first of a class which mounted fifteen 6·1-inch guns instead of her predecessors' ten 8-inch. She had very powerful engines (152,000 shaft horse-power, compared to the 100,000 of the 10,000-ton U.S.S. *Brooklyn*, which was designed to match her). In order to improve stability while giving some extra protection, it was decided to fit her with external bulges, which reduced her speed to about thirty-five knots, still very fast for a cruiser. Her side armour was five inches thick at its maximum, and the deck armour was one and a half inches.

In the late thirties the proponents of the 'big gun' gained the upper hand in Japan, and there was an unwise reversion to the 8-inch gun cruiser. The five triple 6-inch turrets of the *Mogami* class were accordingly replaced by five twin 8-inch turrets. Nothing was said about this; presumably it was hoped to present a nasty shock to Japan's naval enemies. The anti-aircraft armament remained the same at eight 5-inch dual-purpose guns, with numerous automatic 25-mm and 13-mm weapons. In common with other cruisers, a strong torpedo armament, of twelve tubes firing the long-range 24-inch torpedo, was fitted. By this time the displace-ment was around 13,000 tons, and the crew numbered about 850.

At the beginning of the war the *Mogami* was with the Japanese southern group, operating in support of the invasion of the East Indies. She participated in the Battle of the Java Sea, in which Allied cruisers were badly defeated by gunfire and torpedoes. A few days later she was covering the unloading of Japanese transports near the Sunda Straits off Java. The cruisers U.S.S. *Houston* and H.M.A.S. *Perth*, seeking to escape southwards through the straits, came upon this Japanese concentration unexpectedly. They were first attacked by Japanese destroyers, whose torpedoes missed and struck a Japanese transport. The two fugitives then opened fire and managed to sink four transports out of fifty-six, causing the Japanese commanding general to pass twenty minutes in the water, clinging to a piece of wood. But soon the *Mogami* and *Mikuma* came up, and other ships too, and their concentrated gunfire quickly sank the two intruding cruisers. Then, in mid-1942, with her three sister ships, the *Mogami* took part in the Battle of Midway. After the loss of the Japanese carriers, the four cruisers were ordered to close in and bombard Midway Island. However, this order was cancelled and as the four ships changed course they noticed the U.S. submarine *Tambor*, which had been unobtrusively observing them and reporting their presence. This sighting disturbed the Japanese, but the *Mogami* was slow to receive the signal for an emergency turn to avoid possible torpedoes. As a result she collided with her sister the *Mikuma*, smashing her bow and rupturing one of the *Mikuma*'s fuel tanks. Both ships had to reduce speed and were left behind by their consorts, who were hurrying to get out of range of U.S. air attacks. With the *Mikuma* trailing oil, it was not long before the damaged pair was located by the Americans. Twelve dive bombers from Midway attacked, but strong anti-aircraft defence prevented them from scoring any hits. However, one American pilot, giving the Japanese a lesson in suicide tactics, crashed his plane onto the *Mikuma*,

causing some damage. The next day aircraft from the U.S. carrier *Enterprise* made more bombing attacks, sinking the *Mikuma*. The *Mogami* was hit four times. One bomb entered her aftermost turret, killing all inside it, while another entered a boiler room, blocking the escape of about a hundred men who were subsequently burned to death. U.S. Army B-17 bombers were also sent from Midway to bomb the cruiser, but mistook the submarine U.S.S. *Grayling* for their target; they claimed to have sunk the cruiser but this claim was disputed a few days later when the indignant *Grayling* returned to harbour. The *Mogami* managed to limp back home, but was out of service until the following year. When she emerged from the repair yards she was once more a changed ship. Her two after turrets had been removed and replaced by accommodation and catapults for no fewer than eleven seaplanes.

In her new guise, the *Mogami* in late 1943 was part of a Japanese force sent south to attack American transports in the Solomons campaign. While preparing for battle she was attacked in

The Mogami *running her trials in 1935*

the harbour of Rabaul by U.S. carrier aircraft, and again damaged. However, she was repaired in time to take part in the Leyte Gulf operations. In this battle the *Mogami* accompanied the two ill-fated battleships of the Centre Force. After the *Yamashiro* and *Fuso* had been sunk in the night action of Surigao Strait the *Mogami*, already damaged by gunfire, turned and retired back down the strait. Here she encountered a supporting force of Japanese cruisers. Burning and slow-moving, the *Mogami* was thought to have stopped, and this mistake caused the cruiser *Nachi* to collide with her. Thus for the second time in her career the *Mogami* was in collision during a disastrous battle. But this time she did not escape. She was harried by U.S. cruisers, destroyers and carrier aircraft and was eventually scuttled. Unlike the *Mikuma*'s crew, of which more than a thousand had died with their ship, the *Mogami*'s crew was taken off before the end, and lived to fight another day.

U.S.S. BOISE

In the thirties American cruiser design was influenced above all by the desire to match whatever Japan was doing. Thus when it became clear that the Japanese were introducing cruisers mounting no fewer than fifteen 6-inch guns it was not long before the U.S. Navy followed suit. The result was the *Brooklyn* class, built specifically as a reply to Japan's *Mogami*. U.S.S. *Boise* was the sixth of this nine-ship class.

As with the *Mogami*, the reversion to 6-inch guns from the previously favoured 8-inch did not result in a smaller ship. Instead, the Washington Treaty limitation of 10,000 tons was fully utilized by mounting two extra turrets. With five triple turrets, fifteen 6-inch weapons could be mounted, although the third turret had a somewhat restricted field of fire. Eight 5-inch guns provided the heavy anti-aircraft defence, supplemented by automatic weapons whose number was increased during the war. Speed was about thirty-two knots, and with 2,200 tons of fuel the radius of action at the economical speed of fifteen knots was around 14,500 miles. The design was interesting in that the 608-foot hull was flush-decked, and the extra height thus gained was utilized at the stern by a capacious aircraft hangar. The latter, equipped with an elevator, could accommodate no fewer than six planes (although four was normal), and the catapult and crane were placed above it. This location of the aircraft was repeated in subsequent U.S. ships. The armour protection included a maximum of four inches of plate on the side and a 3-inch layer on the main deck, the latter being supplemented in places by $2\frac{1}{2}$-inch armour on the lower deck.

This design set the fashion for subsequent U.S. cruisers. When a reversion was made to the 8-inch gun cruiser the prototype, *Wichita*, was virtually a *Brooklyn* with nine 8-inch instead of fifteen 6-inch guns, and from the *Wichita* was derived the war-built *Baltimore* class. The 6-inch gun cruisers which followed the *Brooklyn*s (the *Cleveland* class) were similarly a development of their predecessors, the main difference being that the third main turret was eliminated, allowing a stronger anti-aircraft armament to be fitted.

At the beginning of the war the *Boise* with two other cruisers was the nucleus of the rather weak U.S. Asiatic Fleet, based in the Philippines. Soon after the Japanese landings in the Philippines these ships retired to the Dutch East Indies and in late January two cruisers with four old destroyers attacked a Japanese convoy preparing to land troops in Borneo. Before action commenced one of the cruisers withdrew with engine trouble, while the *Boise* struck an uncharted rock. The destroyers managed to sink four transports and an escort. Although the mishap to the *Boise* prevented her taking part in this action the resulting need to send her away for repair meant that she escaped the fate of other Allied cruisers defending the East Indies.

In October 1942 the *Boise* was at the Battle of Cape Esperance, which in a sense was the U.S. Navy's revenge for the Battle of Savo Island, which had taken place in the same waters. At night, a column of four U.S. cruisers and five destroyers encountered in the most favourable situation a Japanese force of three cruisers and two destroyers; the Americans were in line ahead and passing at right angles to the advancing Japanese line. This crossing of the enemy's 'T' was always the most sought-after deployment, because it enabled a column to direct all its guns on the leading enemy ships, which themselves could bring only their forward guns and most advanced ships into the battle. On this occasion the Americans and Japanese got themselves into this position quite accidentally. The U.S. admiral was aboard the cruiser *San Francisco*, which did not have the latest radar, while, for once, the Japanese experience in night operations had not enabled them to detect the close presence of their enemy. The *Boise* had good radar but it was misused. After the Americans had opened fire on the surprised Japanese, the cruiser's search radar located a target and the searchlights were unwisely switched on and directed towards the position indicated by radar. As the Russian fleet had learned at the Battle of Tsushima in 1905, the main effect of using searchlights is to draw the enemy's fire, and the *Boise* was soon overwhelmed by a shower of shells. A U.S. scout plane saw a spurt of orange flame shoot up over the *Boise* as an 8-inch shell penetrated her forward turret. Another shell propelled flames through the interior passages into the two forward turrets, incinerating many men. The order to flood the magazines could not be carried out because the men responsible were dead. Fortunately, sea water entering through penetrations had the desired effect. The *Boise*'s consort the *Salt Lake City* then interposed herself, saving the former from further damage. It was later concluded that the one Japanese cruiser (the *Furutaka*) sunk in this battle had been a victim of gunfire from the *Boise* and *Salt Lake City*. The *Boise* returned to the U.S.A. for repair, where at least one newspaper gave her all the credit for the victory, referring to her as a 'one-ship task force'. This comment was not well received on board the other cruisers which had taken part.

She next appeared in the Mediterranean, and her heavy gun armament was invaluable in

U.S.S. Boise *lies off San Pedro, California, at the end of the war*

support of the invasion of Sicily. On two successive days her gunfire broke up enemy tank formations which were advancing towards the weakly defended American beachhead. Later, in the Salerno operations, the *Boise* was sent to relieve her sister ship the *Savannah*, which had lost part of her bottom on being hit by a German glider bomb. Fortunately, soon after the *Boise* took up her bombardment duties it was realized that the airborne radio operators controlling these bombs could be frustrated by smoke screens.

The *Boise* was back in the Pacific in time to take part in the Battle for Leyte Gulf. When the Japanese Centre Force encountered the U.S. battleships and cruisers in the Surigao Strait the *Boise* and *Phoenix* harried the battleship *Yamashiro*. As so many other ships were directing their fire on this unfortunate ship it is impossible to know how accurate and destructive the *Boise*'s guns were on this occasion. It was only a matter of minutes before the *Yamashiro* disintegrated. This was the *Boise*'s last major battle. She was scrapped in 1951, but six of her sisters were transferred to the navies of Argentine, Brazil and Chile. Probably because of their heavy gun armament, these ships were attractive to South American admirals, and most of them were still in service in the seventies.

H.M.S. AJAX

In the short interval between the disenchantment with the 8-inch gun cruiser and the adoption of the big 6-inch gun cruiser Britain built three classes of the type of cruiser she really wanted, the small 6-inch gun ship. First came the *Leander* class of about 7,000 tons, mounting eight 6-inch guns. Then came the *Amphion* class which was very similar, except that a rearrangement of the boilers entailed the provision of two funnels in place of the large trunked funnel of the *Leander*s. Lastly came the *Arethusa* class, true light cruisers of less than 6,000 tons and mounting six 6-inch guns. All three of these classes were invaluable during the war. The *Arethusa* and *Penelope* of the *Arethusa* class gained great distinction, the *Penelope* being nicknamed H.M.S. *Pepperpot* on account of the multiple penetrations she received during the Mediterranean campaign. H.M.A.S. *Sydney* of the *Amphion* class earned fame by routing two Italian cruisers and later was in action with a disguised German raider, an action in which both ships were sunk. Of the *Leander* class, it was the *Ajax* which won most glory, although all five ships had an active life.

H.M.S. *Ajax* gained worldwide fame in December 1939, when she was the flagship of Commodore Harwood, leading a group hunting the 'pocket battleship' *Graf Spee* in the South Atlantic. In this group were the *Exeter* (six 8-inch guns) and the two 6-inch gun sister ships *Ajax* and *Achilles*, the last being a New Zealand ship. Harwood had anticipated that the *Graf Spee* would next appear off the River Plate and he had decided that his cruisers, should they sight her, would attack by day or by night. In this attack they would act as two units: the *Exeter* with her heavier guns would attack alone on one flank while the two 6-inch gun cruisers would stay on the other flank with their gunfire concentrated (that is, both cruisers' guns would be directed from the *Ajax*).

When battle was joined the *Graf Spee* soon concentrated her fire on the *Exeter*, causing great damage. After making a courageous but unsuccessful torpedo attack, the *Exeter* was forced to break off after about half an hour of battle. Meanwhile the *Ajax* and *Achilles*, whose gunfire had been accurate but not especially damaging at eleven miles, closed in. To avoid possible torpedoes the Germans turned away, losing the chance to bring a damaging fire on these two cruisers while the *Exeter* was still out of action. Then, as the *Ajax* and *Achilles* zigzagged and laid smoke to escape the German 11-inch shells, the *Exeter*, with just her two after guns still serviceable, returned to the fray. The *Graf Spee* once again turned the 11-inch guns onto her and after fifteen minutes the British cruiser, listing perceptibly and with only one gun still firing, withdrew for the last time. But by now the two smaller British cruisers had moved in to within five miles range and, although they once more came under damaging fire from the 11-inch guns, succeeded in inflicting significant damage. When the *Ajax* had only three guns serviceable, and only one-fifth of her ammunition left, the two cruisers withdrew and adopted a shadowing role.

Luckily, the two battered cruisers were not called upon to renew the battle, for the *Graf Spee* was scuttled a few days later, after seeking refuge in Montevideo. This naval victory, their first in the war, brought great encouragement to the British. In retrospect, the euphoria was somewhat exaggerated: the portrayal by the press of the action as a David and Goliath combat was unfair, in that it failed to note that there were three Davids and only half a Goliath. All the same, it is hard to see how Commodore Harwood and his crews could have dealt with their powerful enemy more intelligently or more courageously. Technically, an interesting feature was that the two light cruisers had not suffered unduly from the lightness of their armour. When built they had been criticized on the ground that their armour was insufficient protection against other cruisers; it was thin, patchy, and the deck was only one and a half inches thick at its maximum. Yet there had been no fatal penetrations, and later in the war

other ships of the type proved able to survive heavy punishment. The only member of the *Leander* class to be sunk, the *Neptune*, struck no fewer than four mines. The *Sydney*, in its final engagement, may have been sunk by penetrations in its vital parts, but even this is not certain, because no survivors lived to tell the tale.

After the Battle of the River Plate the *Ajax* was repaired and then sent to the Mediterranean. She was with the cruisers at the Battle of Cape Matapan and took part in the evacuation of Greece, conveying several thousand British soldiers to Egypt. Soon afterwards, with her sister ship *Orion* and the new light cruiser *Dido* and four destroyers, she intercepted a night convoy carrying German troops for an invasion of Crete. One of the torpedo boat escorts was sunk, and many troop-carrying craft. German troop losses were very heavy, and their seaborne invasion of Crete was completely ruined. Heavy air attacks were made on some British ships when daylight came, but the *Ajax* was untouched. A week later, during the evacuation of Crete, the *Ajax* came under heavy air attack. Again a number of ships were sunk or badly damaged, but not the *Ajax*. In May 1942 she was again in action, supporting by shore bombardment the British army's advance in Syria. But on New Year's Day of 1943 her luck changed and she was badly damaged by bombing while supporting the Allied forces in Algeria. Repaired once more, she took part in the Italian campaign and also

H.M.S. Ajax *supporting the Normandy landings with her main guns*

assisted loyal Greek sailors at Alexandria to board three Free Greek ships, whose crews had mutinied in support of the demand for communist participation in the Greek government in exile.

Recalled from the Mediterranean to take part in the invasion of Normandy, on D-Day the *Ajax* was one of four light cruisers which carried out the preliminary bombardment for the 'Gold' landing. Apparently this gunfire was very effective, for the German batteries offered little resistance to the landing. After these duties, the *Ajax* returned to the Mediterranean in time to participate in the liberation of Greece. The departure of the Germans from Greece was immediately followed by a communist uprising, and British forces were used to keep this rising in check until a general election could be held. Thus at many points the British and the local communists came into opposition. The Royal Navy helped by landing Royal Marine bands and football teams and, if these failed to pacify, by bombardment. Meanwhile the mutual repulsion between the Greek Prime Minister, newly arrived from London, and Greece's spiritual leader, Archbishop Damaskinos, led Winston Churchill to arrange a meeting between himself and these two Greeks on board the *Ajax*. By mischance, the two Greeks arrived at the quay at the same time,

The Ajax *and* Achilles *cruise off the River Plate after the engagement with the* Graf Spee. *The blistered paint of the 6-in. guns is one consequence of that action*

and had to share the available space in the *Ajax*'s boat. On boarding, the Archbishop was hastily shunted into the admiral's cabin while the Prime Minister went to see Churchill. It was Christmas Day, and no sooner had the bearded, cloaked and staff-bearing archbishop entered the cabin than a troop of sailors in fancy dress arrived to sing carols to the admiral. The Archbishop, apparently, had some difficulty in convincing people that he too was not a sailor in fancy dress.

For some of her officers, this comedy was the climax of the ship's career. She claimed the headlines only once again, when after the war it was rumoured that she was to be sold to a South American navy. Churchill, then in opposition, produced a fine show of indignation at this proposal. In the end she was scrapped. Her sister the *Achilles*, however, lives on as the *Delhi* of the Indian navy.

H.M.S. BELFAST

Britain's reply to the *Mogami* class cruisers was the *Southampton* class, a very successful design which mounted twelve 6-inch guns instead of the six or eight of the preceding light cruisers. These ships were also better protected, with side armour of a maximum thickness of four inches; it was held that a big 6-inch gun cruiser should be able to withstand shells fired at long range by 8-inch gun cruisers (yet another of those theoretical considerations which determined design but had little relevance to what actually happened in wartime). Another feature of the *Southampton*s was the two hangars alongside the first funnel, and the catapult athwartships at this position; this enabled the aircraft to be kept away from sea water contamination, and to run directly onto the catapult without lifting.

The last two of the *Southampton*s, the *Edin-*burgh and the *Belfast*, were built to a revised design. A rearrangement of machinery, boiler, and magazine spaces was undertaken, the new internal disposition being externally evident from the rather unattractive positioning of the funnels. The fighting qualities were marginally enhanced by the provision of twelve instead of eight 4-inch anti-aircraft guns, and by better armour. Officially the displacement (standard) was 10,000 tons, but the design displacement was closer to 11,000. After wartime changes the final standard displacement was about 11,500 tons, with an overall length of 613 feet. The Admiralty's preference for reliable rather than sophisticated machinery meant that the boilers

The Belfast, *wearing her wartime 'dazzle' paint*

worked at the moderate pressure of 350 lbs per square inch, to drive turbines producing 80,000 shaft horsepower and thirty-two knots.

Launched by Mrs Neville Chamberlain at Belfast in 1938, H.M.S. *Belfast* was completed just in time for the war. In late 1939 she was based in Scotland and intercepted three German blockade-runners, of which the most important was the liner *Cap Norte*, carrying German reservists from South America. But in November, in the Firth of Forth, her hull was badly distorted by one of the first magnetic mines to be encountered. Repairs really amounted to a rebuilding, and she did not rejoin the fleet until late 1942. Like her sister the *Edinburgh* (which had been torpedoed and sunk in 1942), she spent most of her wartime life in northern waters, covering convoys to Russia. It was

while covering one such convoy in December 1943 that the *Belfast* played a key role in the destruction of the *Scharnhorst*.

Leading two other cruisers (the *Norfolk* and

In Arctic service. The foredeck of the Belfast, *with the encrusted 6-in. guns laid ready for action on either beam*

the *Sheffield*) the *Belfast* was ordered to close an eastbound convoy to protect it from the *Scharnhorst*, which had left its base in northern Norway. Being recently returned to service, the *Belfast* carried the latest radar equipment, and this picked up an echo from the German battleship at 25,000 yards. When the range was down to about 13,000 yards the *Norfolk* opened fire. She hit the *Scharnhorst* with a shell which failed to explode and by measuring this shell the Germans, who could see little in the Arctic twilight, concluded that they were being attacked by cruisers. Another shell from the *Norfolk* put much of the German radar out of action, a vital success. Because of the high seas the cruisers could not keep up with the *Scharnhorst*, and therefore went towards the convoy in the expectation that the Germans still intended to attack it. About two hours later the *Belfast*'s radar did indeed pick up the enemy, and this news was radioed to the battleship *Duke of York*, which was approaching the scene of action. Meanwhile the cruisers exchanged fire with the Germans for about twenty minutes, both sides receiving some damage. The *Scharnhorst* then retired and the cruisers shadowed her, keeping the Germans out of sight but within the *Belfast*'s radar range. In this way the *Duke of York* was enabled to encounter the *Scharnhorst* and engage her with gunfire. In the final stage, the *Belfast* was once again in action when she and the *Norfolk* opened fire to prevent the *Scharnhorst* escaping to the north. The crippled German battleship finally sank after torpedo attacks by destroyers. In this engagement the *Belfast* had fired 316 6-inch and seventy-seven 4-inch shells.

Six months later, the *Belfast* was off Normandy as part of the bombarding force; between 6 and 14 June she fired almost 2,000 rounds, mainly against German batteries opposing the 3rd Canadian Division. This was virtually the end of her war service. In the postwar period she took part in shore bombardments during the Korean War and was later modernized; externally the main result of this modernization was the replacement of tripod by lattice masts. She went into reserve in 1963, but in 1971 was permanently berthed in the Pool of London as a museum ship.

THE PRINZ EUGEN

Because of treaty restrictions, Germany did not build 8-inch gun cruisers until the late thirties. Then she laid down a class of five. The *Prinz Eugen* was the third of these, and her design was modified in the light of experience gained with the first two, the *Admiral Hipper* and the *Blücher*. The final pair was never completed, so the *Prinz Eugen* can be regarded as the final development of the German heavy cruiser.

These ships, which well exceeded their nominal 10,000-ton displacement, carried eight 8-inch guns in four turrets, and a heavy anti-aircraft armament of twelve 4·1-inch dual-purpose weapons. Armour was average for this kind of ship, with the waterline belt $3\frac{1}{4}$ inches at its thickest part and horizontal armour varying from $1\frac{1}{4}$ to $3\frac{3}{4}$ inches. Internal subdivision was carefully thought out, and there were external anti-torpedo bulges. The propulsion was highly developed. All three ships had unusual boilers (the *Prinz Eugen* had Lamont boilers with a maximum pressure of no less than 1,012 lbs per square inch). Three sets of geared turbines developed a nominal 132,000 shaft horsepower, giving thirty-two knots. But in contriving ultra-sophisticated machinery, the designers neglected one or two simple matters. In 1941, for example, when the *Prinz Eugen* was operating in warm Atlantic waters, it was discovered that her condensers could not convert her exhaust steam fast enough into boiler feedwater.

Her baptism of fire came in July 1940, while she was still being completed. During an R.A.F. raid she was struck by a bomb which, said the cynics, had been aimed at Kiel's railway station. She commissioned the following month and in May 1941 made her first foray, accompanying the *Bismarck* into the North Atlantic. With her consort she engaged H.M.S. *Hood* and H.M.S. *Prince of Wales*, scoring hits on both and remaining undamaged herself. Soon after the sinking of the *Hood* and the disengagement of the *Prince of Wales*, the *Prinz Eugen* quietly separated from the *Bismarck* and went hunting for convoys in the Atlantic. She was unsuccessful, and soon had to go to Brest because of condenser trouble. For eight months she remained there, with the *Scharnhorst* and the *Gneisenau*. Constant air raids and continual R.A.F. reconnaissance made fresh excursions into the Atlantic difficult, and in February 1942 the three ships made their famous 'Channel dash'. With strong air and small craft escort,

The Prinz Eugen. *Below : at sea. Left : After Germany's surrender unloading her ammunition at Copenhagen. Right : In action against British aircraft during the 'Channel dash'*

the three heavy units hurried up the English Channel towards Germany. Owing to a combination of misfortune and negligence the R.A.F. failed to discover the departure of the ships from Brest until it was too late to do much about it. The Germans passed unscathed within sight of Dover. Heroic and often suicidal air attacks produced no results, and a torpedo attack by five old destroyers was beaten off; the *Prinz Eugen*'s guns damaged H.M.S. *Worcester* in this engagement. Thus the *Prinz Eugen* arrived safely at the Elbe. This singeing of the British navy's beard was a great propaganda asset for the Germans; the British tacitly acknowledged this by setting up a commission of enquiry, which published its report four years later.

But a week later the *Prinz Eugen*'s stern was blown off by a torpedo from the British submarine *Trident*. She was out of service for eight months, and then went to the Baltic. Here she supported the German troops in their various withdrawals on the Russian front. During these operations she rammed the light cruiser *Leipzig* amidships. The two ships were

locked together for fourteen hours, and the *Leipzig* took no further part in the war. In April 1945, with the Russian advance threatening the security of the Baltic, the *Prinz Eugen* went to Copenhagen and it was here, on the German surrender, that she was handed over to the Allies. She was allocated as reparations to the U.S.A., which used her as a target in the Bikini atomic bomb tests of 1946.

Thus the *Prinz Eugen*, although she became well known, really did very little for the German war effort. Her sister ships did even less: the *Blücher* was sunk by Norwegian coastal defences in 1940 and the *Hipper*'s record as a raider was uninspiring. Part of their trouble was unreliable machinery, and part was their comparatively short range. Their design had been influenced by the supposed need for ships which could attack convoys taking French African troops to fight in Europe, and which could cope with the French cruisers. As so often happened, designing ships with a specific enemy and purpose in view resulted in units which could not really fulfil the roles which war actually imposed on them.

THE
DESTROYER

Conventionally described as the 'maid of all work', the destroyer might perhaps be better regarded as the most powerful of the unarmoured ships. Its speed, manoeuvrability and torpedo armament made it capable of sinking larger ships, while with its gun armament it could cope with ships of its own size. It was fairly cheap, could be built in large numbers, and was therefore worth risking in perilous enterprises. During the First World War it acquired a new role, that of submarine hunter.

With so many roles to fill, a perfect destroyer was unobtainable. Designers were probably hindered more than helped by the staff requirements which were handed down to them. Some admirals still regarded the destroyer as primarily a torpedo ship, others felt that it should have a more powerful gun armament, others gave it a minesweeping and minelaying role, while a few of the more far-sighted pointed out that it should have a strong anti-aircraft defence. All demanded high speed. Some countries solved their design problems by building ever-larger destroyers, but others could not do this. Britain, for example, was limited by treaty to 150,000 tons of destroyers and realized that if her ships were more than about 1,500 tons each she would not be able to build enough of them.

British designers therefore endeavoured to cram as much equipment into their hulls as possible, without creating too much topweight. Destroyer commanders complained ceaselessly of the arrangement and design of their ships: some designs rolled badly; others pitched too much; bridges were too cramped; smoke blew into the commanders' eyes. The British genius for crude plumbing was expressed in a veritable snakes' honeymoon of intertwining pipework. In heavy weather guns were engulfed, and the sea found its way below deck into the mess spaces. On the other hand, it is probable that the British destroyers were the most seaworthy; unlike the Americans and Russians, the British lost no destroyers from storm damage.

Nevertheless, the British destroyer, on paper, compared badly with those of other countries. In the late twenties and thirties it was customary to build a flotilla of nine ships each year. These were of a standard pattern, only detail alterations being made year by year. These vessels (classes A, B, C, D, E, F, G, H and I) were twin-funnelled craft with unexciting but reliable machinery designed to produce thirty-six knots. The main armament was four single 4·7-inch guns and from eight to ten torpedo tubes. Other nations were building destroyers with a heavier gun armament: the Japanese had destroyers mounting six 5-inch guns while the French 'super-destroyers' mounted 5·5-inch guns and could reach forty knots. The French ships were, however, almost double the size of the British.

Foreign competition persuaded the British Admiralty to build sixteen destroyers in which the torpedo armament was halved and the gun armament doubled. These, the *Tribal* class, had eight 4·7-inch guns and four tubes. However, this experiment was not

Top: U.S.S. *Heerman* rushes headlong into her last battle: in action against Japanese battleships at Leyte Gulf

Bottom: The *Richard Beitzen*, a pre-war German destroyer, carrying five 5-in. guns

Previous pages: U.S.S. *Shaw*, a pre-war destroyer with a heavy torpedo armament. Three of her four sets of torpedo tubes, disposed around the after funnel, can clearly be discerned

repeated. Instead, the next five series of destroyers were a compromise (J, K, L, M and N classes). Their hull structure and machinery were different from previous designs, allowing among other things one large funnel to replace the previous two. They carried tcn torpedo tubes and six 4·7-inch guns in three twin mounts. Thus both the advocates of heavier gun armaments and the torpedo school were satisfied, although at the cost of a somewhat high displacement. However, such destroyers were too valuable to use on escort duties and moreover offered little defence against aircraft. Both these drawbacks were only partly solved by the construction of the small escort destroyers of the *Hunt* class. Whereas the U.S.A. and Japan were already using dual-purpose 5-inch guns, the introduction of dual-purpose guns into the Royal Navy destroyers met much opposition. It was correctly argued that it was impossible to design a gun which could be easily loaded at angles of elevation from minus ten degrees to eighty degrees; therefore a dual-purpose gun would suffer from a reduced rate of fire. It was also said that there were manufacturing problems involved (which was true, but they were surmountable). It was not said, because it was not widely realized, that even with guns capable of high elevation the anti-aircraft defence would be weak unless gunnery direction equipment was at least as sophisticated for anti-aircraft work as it was for surface action. By the late thirties the Admiralty had compromised by fitting guns which elevated to forty degrees instead of thirty degrees, but this was of little help. During the war, therefore, many destroyers were given a heavy anti-aircraft gun in place of one set of torpedo tubes and even the proud *Tribals* sacrificed a pair of surface guns for a pair of 4-inch anti-aircraft weapons. It was not until the close of the war that destroyers entered service with four 4·5-inch dual-purpose weapons.

When America entered the war she had about 200 destroyers, but half of these were of the old four-funnel design built under the First World War programmes. In the interwar period several quite varied designs had been built, varying from 1,500 to 1,900 tons. These carried from four to eight 5-inch guns and from eight to sixteen torpedo tubes. Top speeds were about thirty-six knots and range of action about 6,000 miles. These last two figures corresponded closely to British performance; the apparently superior fighting qualities of the U.S. ships were attained partly through an acceptance of more topweight and partly through the use of higher boiler pressures (600 lbs in some cases, double the British rating). Thanks to the great variety of U.S. designs, when war approached it was possible to launch a programme of mass destroyer construction embodying the best features of the preceding designs; during the war no fewer than 417 destroyers were built of the *Bristol*, *Fletcher*, *Sumner* and *Gearing* classes.

The Japanese, too, had a good basis for wartime construction. This was the *Kagero* class, of about 2,000 tons and mounting six 5-inch dual-purpose guns and eight torpedo tubes. War-built destroyers were very similar. A feature of the Japanese destroyers was not only their long-range 24-inch torpedoes, but their ability to reload their torpedo tubes on the move (other nations' destroyers carried only a one-shot torpedo armament). During the war, as with other countries' destroyers, extra light anti-aircraft guns were shipped, as well as radar.

The German destroyers were few, but were supported by torpedo boats (in effect, small destroyers). At first fairly conventional and reliable designs were favoured, mounting five 5-inch guns. But later the Germans fell into the temptation of building large destroyers with 5·9-inch guns. These cruiser-size weapons made the ships top-heavy and poor sea boats, and moreover had a rate of fire much inferior to the 4·7-inch guns of British destroyers. In the short sharp engagements of the North Sea these German 'super-destroyers' were not therefore very successful.

Italian destroyers were of moderate size and they, too, were supplemented by torpedo boats. They were fast and carried moderate gun armaments of 4·7-inch guns. They did not distinguish themselves in the war, although the Italians did prove good submarine-hunters. Like the French, the Italians claimed high speeds for their cruisers and destroyers, often allowing them to run their trials with a following wind and tide. In the view of the British Admiralty, this was done to attract foreign buyers for Italian ships, and Whitehall accordingly suggested to British destroyer-builders that similar trials should be held of selected new British destroyers. But nothing came of this, partly because the British shipbuilders, with their refined commercial acumen,

DESTROYER TYPES OF THE SECOND WORLD WAR

	Years of completion	Tonnage	Main guns	Torpedo tubes	Nominal speed (knots)
Old types					
V and W class (Britain)	1917–18	1,100	4 4-in	6	34
4-funnellers (U.S.A.)	1919–21	1,100	4 4-in	12	35
Interwar types					
A, B, C, D, E, F, G, H and I classes (Britain)	1930–40	1,400	4 4·7-in	8 or 10	36
Tribal class (Britain)	1938–9	1,900	8 4·7-in	4	36
J, K, L, M and N classes (Britain)	1939–42	1,700–1,950	6 4·7-in	8 or 10	36
Hunt class (Britain)	1940–3	1,000	4 or 6 4-in D.P.	0 or 2	27
Selfridge class (U.S.A.)	1936–7	1,850	8 5-in D.P.	8	37
Mahan class (U.S.A.)	1936–7	1,500	5 5-in D.P.	12	36
Gridley class (U.S.A.)	1938–40	1,500	4 5-in D.P.	16	36
Benson and *Bristol* classes (U.S.A.)	1940–3	1,650	4 5-in D.P.	10	36
Kagero class (Japan)	1939–41	2,000	6 5-in D.P.	8	35
Z-1 class (Germany)	1938–9	2,400	5 5-in	8	38
Aviere class (Italy)	1938–9	1,650	4 4·7-in	6	39
Mogador class (France)	1938	2,900	8 5·5-in	10	38
War-built types					
O and P classes (Britain)	1941–2	1,550	4 4-in	8	34
Q, R, S, T, U, V and W classes (Britain)	1942–4	1,750	4 4·7-in	8	34
Fletcher class (U.S.A.)	1942–4	2,100	5 5-in D.P.	10	35
Geary and *Sumner* classes (U.S.A.)	1944–5	2,200	6 5-in D.P.	10	36
Z-31 class (Germany)	1942–3	2,600	5 5·9-in	8	38
T-22 class (Germany)	1942–4	1,300	4 4·1-in D.P.	6	33

Many units of the U.S. Navy's well known but elderly four-funnelled destroyers were transferred to Allied navies. Here a Canadian 'four-stacker' is shown on Atlantic convoy duty

DESTROYER STRENGTHS AND DESTROYER LOSSES

	Britain	France	Netherlands	U.S.S.R.	U.S.A.	Germany	Italy	Japan
Total at time of entry into war	168	59	10	72	199	41	59	110
Units completed during war	212	0	1	7	417	47	7	66
War losses	154	39	11	33	101	62	55	140

N.B. British figures include the *Hunt* class, but U.S. figures exclude destroyer escorts. German figures include destroyers officially classed as torpedo boats.

demanded that the Admiralty should contribute the extra insurance premium which would be needed to cover trials carried out well above the designed horsepowers. In the end, the Italians did succeed in winning foreign interest. The Soviet navy in the late thirties based its new cruisers and destroyers on Italian designs and built fast ships which, not surprisingly, were quite unsuitable for northern waters. At least one of the destroyers broke up in a gale.

Destroyers were so numerous, and took part in so many actions, that several volumes would be needed to describe their work. Indicative of their role are the totals of their losses. The U.S. Navy lost 101 destroyers, while the British and Commonwealth navies lost 154, a rate of loss somewhat slower than the American, the 154 being spread over a war two years longer than America's war. Axis losses are not strictly comparable, due to the high rate of loss in the final weeks of the war when small ships were at the mercy of massive air attacks; neither Germany nor Japan emerged from the war with more than a handful of serviceable destroyers. For Britain, it was the Mediterranean which proved most lethal for her destroyers, and it was the aircraft, followed by the submarine, which proved to be the destroyer's worst enemy. British destroyers suffered heavy losses in the evacuations of France and Greece, but their work in these crises was vital, many ships managing to cram 1,400 men into their small dimensions. The Japanese also used destroyers as troop-carriers, both in advance and retreat.

Of the classic destroyer versus destroyer actions, those of Narvik in 1940 and of the Solomon Islands in 1943 were outstanding. In the Norwegian fiords five H class destroyers harrying German transports encountered five German destroyers and both sides lost two ships. The British then sent a stronger force into Narvik Fiord, supported by a battleship, and sank eight additional German destroyers. In the Solomon Islands campaign neither the Japanese nor the American destroyers were handled as well as they might have been: officers of both sides seemed slow to work out the best tactics for these confused night actions. The result all too often was that ships fired at their own consorts, or collided with them, or refrained from blowing their enemies out of the water in the belief that they were friendly ships. However, six American destroyers won a commendable victory at the Battle of Vella Gulf, sinking three out of four Japanese destroyers which they had surprised. But a few days later three U.S. destroyers after an initial success against six Japanese rather needlessly ran into torpedoes fired by the latter and were lucky to lose only one ship. At the Battle of Cape St George soon afterwards it was two Japanese destroyers which, all unsuspecting, were sent to the bottom by a night torpedo attack.

Destroyer successes in David and Goliath battles included the classic daytime attack (described on p. 118) made by U.S.S. *Johnston* and two other destroyers on a Japanese force which included three battleships and several cruisers. The British

H.M.S. *Onslow*, a hastily built 'utility' destroyer which distinguished herself in action with German heavy ships

equivalent of this bold action was the defence of a Russian convoy by H.M.S. *Onslow* and four other destroyers. Using their guns, and threatening to make torpedo attacks behind smoke screens, these small craft held off a German force consisting of six destroyers, the cruiser *Hipper*, and the 'pocket battleship' *Lützow*. The poor performance of the German force drove Hitler into one of his celebrated rages, the German commander-in-chief (Raeder) was replaced by Dönitz, and Hitler ordered the withdrawal from service of the big ships, an order which was modified only after much persuasion by Dönitz.

Destroyers had been expected to make attacks on bigger ships only at night or in poor visibility, and such attacks were in fact made from time to time. One of the most successful was the sinking of two Italian cruisers by four destroyers (the *Maori* and the *Sikh* of the *Tribal* class, *Legion* of the L class, and the Royal Dutch Navy *Isaac Sweers*). The destroyers crept in at night between the North African coast and the Italian *Giussano* and *Barbiano*. Being invisible against the dark coast, they launched their torpedoes and then hurried off unscathed. A parallel German success was the sinking by two torpedo boats of the British cruiser *Charybdis* and a destroyer; the British force, consisting of the cruiser and six destroyers, was taken by surprise in this night action and was unable to retaliate. Italian destroyers, despite their claimed high speed, had no similar achievements; it was the small, fast Italian motor torpedo boats which sank the British cruisers *Manchester* and *York*. In the Pacific war, the night torpedo attacks by one Australian and several U.S. destroyers on the Japanese Southern Force in the Battle for Leyte Gulf resulted in the disintegration of one battleship and damage to a battleship and a cruiser with trifling loss to the attackers; most of the casualties seem to have been the result of 'friendly' gunfire, a form of attack to which destroyers of all nations were very liable.

117

U.S.S. JOHNSTON

The Battle for Leyte Gulf was, by several definitions, the greatest naval battle in history and in it the destroyer *Johnston* played one of the greatest roles. This ship was less than a year old at the time, having been completed in October 1943 as one of the 175 war-built *Fletcher* class. These ships were flush-decked, displaced about 2,100 tons, and were 375 feet in length. On these dimensions they mounted five single 5-inch dual-purpose guns, two twin 40-mm Bofors and four 20-mm Oerlikon light anti-aircraft guns, ten torpedo tubes in quintuple mountings and six depth charge throwers. Boilers worked at 565 lbs per square inch, supplying high temperature steam (850 degrees F.) to turbines capable of producing thirty-five knots. Unlike contemporary British destroyers, the hull was welded; at a slight sacrifice of structural strength, this reduced weight and also speeded production: one of the *Johnston*'s sisters was built in just over five months.

War is a period of unpleasant surprises, and few surprises could have been more unpleasant than that inflicted on the commander of the U.S. escort carriers off the Philippine island of Samar on 25 October 1944. Shortly after sunrise he sighted the massive pagoda-like masts of Japanese battleships on the horizon. The six eighteen-knot carriers hastily turned away and launched whatever aircraft they could, armed with whatever missiles were at hand. These planes had little hope of mounting a successful coordinated attack on the Japanese, but at least they might engage their attention. Meanwhile 14-inch, 16-inch and 18-inch shells began to fall near the carriers. The U.S. commander (Admiral Sprague), not expecting that his vulnerable carriers could last more than a few minutes, radioed desperately for help and meantime ordered his three destroyers to attack the enemy. A chance rain squall then hid him from the Japanese for a few precious minutes.

The *Johnston* was the destroyer nearest to the Japanese, and had already moved towards them, laying a smokescreen. At about 18,000 yards from the leading ship of the Japanese cruiser squadron, she opened fire with her 5-inch guns, despatching about 200 rounds before the Japanese turned their guns on her. Her boilers had not reached full pressure, and she could make only twenty-five knots, but at this speed she pushed closer to the Japanese before turning and launching all ten of her torpedoes at 10,000 yards. One of her torpedoes crippled the leading cruiser, the *Kumano*, whose flag officers had to transfer at this crucial moment into another ship. A few minutes later the *Johnston*, which had so far avoided all shells, was hit by three 14-inch shells from the Japanese battleships, as well as three 6-inch. An eye witness later described this as 'like a puppy being smashed by a truck'. The *Johnston* had to reduce speed, and her guns were put temporarily out of action. Luckily, the same rain squall which had earlier protected the carriers now covered the crippled destroyer for ten valuable minutes.

When the rain cleared the two other destroyers had made their attacks; these are thought to have damaged one or two cruisers, and in addition the flagship *Yamato* was persuaded by fear of torpedoes to reverse course for a vital ten minutes. But the two attacking destroyers had been crippled and would soon be sunk. This left the Americans with three destroyer escorts, small ships never intended for fleet actions but carrying a few torpedoes. These ships went in to make a second attack and were joined by the undefeated *Johnston*. The latter had expended her torpedoes, had lost effective gunnery control, and could not reach full speed, but she nevertheless went into the attack so as to give gun support to the three smaller ships. Amid smoke and rain, manoeuvring violently to avoid cruiser gunfire, the *Johnston* at one point found herself engaged in a gunnery duel at only 7,000 yards with the battleship *Kongo*. The latter's gunnery was no better than it had been earlier in the war, but the *Johnston* claimed to have scored a few hits with her own puny weapons. Next the *Johnston*, seeing the cruiser *Yahagi* and four destroyers advancing to make torpedo attacks on the American carriers, turned her guns on these five ships. The Japanese, not realizing that the *Johnston* had no torpedoes, launched their own torpedoes at the carriers prematurely in order to deal with the troublesome *Johnston*. None of their torpedoes hit the carriers but their concentrated gunfire finally put an end to the gallant *Johnston*. Her commander evacuated his shattered and burning bridge and commanded his ship from the stern, but after many more hits the Abandon Ship order was given. By this time the Japanese, confused and delayed by the destroyer and air attacks, had lost their chance of a great victory. Their guns had mortally damaged one carrier but that was all, and the U.S. destroyers and aircraft had already sent three Japanese cruisers to the bottom. There seems little doubt that the sacrifice of the *Johnston* and her two sisters, with a little help from rain squalls, had saved the day for the Americans.

Of the destroyer's 327-man crew, fifty were killed in the action, forty-five died of wounds while in the water, and ninety-two were lost in the water. The *Johnston*'s commander, whose pugnacity was perhaps inherited from his Red Indian (Cherokee) ancestors, was not among those saved. The survivor who considered himself the luckiest was the man who, before being picked up, had been tasted and rejected by two different sharks.

U.S.S. Johnston *at Seattle shortly after completion. Unlike many wartime pictures, radar gear at the masthead and above the bridge has not been blacked out by the censor*

H.M.S. SAUMAREZ

In the first year of the war Britain began to build large numbers of destroyers under the War Emergency Programme. The disputes within the Admiralty about what weapons a destroyer should carry had not abated, but the need to build as many ships as quickly as possible determined the design of the new ships. In general, they were built to existing patterns and made use of whatever guns were available. Thus the wartime O, P, Q, R, S, T, U, V and W classes were based on the J class, but used 4-inch or 4·7-inch guns in single mountings. Two following classes (Z and C) used the new 4·5-inch gun, but it was not until the *Battle* class, finished too late for the war, that eighty degrees of elevation were allowed to the main guns, making them really suitable for anti-aircraft work.

The S class, of which the *Saumarez* became the most distinguished member, was planned in late 1940, just after Dunkirk had demonstrated the vulnerability of destroyers to air attack and after the Norway campaign had demonstrated that forty-degree elevation of destroyer guns did not make them effective anti-aircraft weapons. Nevertheless, the S class could not be given high angle main weapons: the four 4·7-inch guns which they mounted elevated only to fifty-five degrees. Thanks to a redesigned ammunition hoist, these guns could each fire twelve rounds per minute in favourable conditions. For anti-aircraft defence they had a twin 40-mm Bofors automatic gun with a range of 2,500 yards, laid and controlled by equipment whose prototype the Admiralty had 'discovered' on a Dutch destroyer which had taken refuge in Britain. There were also four 20-mm Oerlikon guns (range 1,000 yards). Eight torpedo tubes were carried, arranged in two sets. The anti-submarine armament was ASDIC (Allied Submarine Detection Investigation Committee, later known as SONAR, Sound Navigation and Ranging) detection equipment, backed by seventy depth charges launched by four depth charge throwers and two sets of dropping rails.

On trials, thirty-one knots was reached on a full load displacement (2,500 tons; standard displacement was 1,750 tons). In time, the displacement of these ships rose as new equipment was added; for example, a few months after completion a lattice mast replaced the tripod in order to carry the extra weight of the latest radar. Range of action was about 4,500 miles at twenty knots.

The *Saumarez* was laid down in September 1941 and completed in July 1943. Like many other destroyers of her generation her completion was delayed by wartime production difficulties. She was attached to the Home Fleet and with three sister ships escorted the battleship *Duke of York* in the hunt for the *Scharnhorst* in late 1943. After the *Duke of York* had scored some hits on the Germans, the four S class destroyers were ordered to attack with torpedoes. Working up to thirty-three knots, they attacked in pairs, two on each flank. The *Savage* and *Saumarez* attracted the Germans' attention on the port side, suffering very little from the 5·9-inch and 4·1-inch barrage, while H.M.S. *Scorpion* and the Norwegian *Stord* moved in to launch sixteen torpedoes at only 2,000 yards. At this stage the *Saumarez* was about 7,000 yards from the enemy, and was engaging her with her three foremost 4·7-inch guns. The *Scharnhorst*, belatedly realizing the torpedo peril, turned away, but this turn brought her into a favourable position for attack by the other pair of destroyers. The *Saumarez* and *Savage* quickly retrained their tubes and turned to fire them as the *Scharnhorst* opened fire on them with all guns. One or two 11-inch shells struck the *Saumarez*, passing through her thin plating without exploding. But some shells landing in the sea nearby threw splinters which killed several men and damaged the starboard engine. Nevertheless the *Saumarez* managed to fire half of her set of torpedoes at 1,800 yards, while the *Savage* fired all eight of hers at 3,500 yards. The *Scharnhorst* appears to have been hit by four torpedoes, one from the first attack and three from the twelve torpedoes

H.M.S. Saumarez, *ready to join the fleet*

despatched by the *Saumarez* and *Savage*. This reduced the battleship's speed and made her end certain.

The *Saumarez* had suffered badly. She was holed, one engine was out of action, and a smoke float stowed aft had been ignited. The resulting smoke was thought to be the result of an internal fire, and the after magazine had accordingly been flooded. However, the ship managed to crawl into a north Russian port for temporary repairs before going home.

When the situation eased in the North Sea the *Saumarez*, like many another Home Fleet ship, was transferred to the Far East. The Royal Navy never succeeded in doing as much damage to the Japanese navy as it had itself suffered from that same navy in 1941 and 1942. Of the Japanese major units, only three heavy cruisers fell victim to British forces. Two of these were submarine victims but the third was destroyed in what will probably remain as the last classical destroyer torpedo attack. The *Saumarez* took a leading part in this action.

The quarry was the cruiser *Haguro* which, accompanied by a destroyer, had been spotted by aircraft making its way from Malaya towards the Indian Ocean Andaman Islands, where it was required to pick up the withdrawing Japanese garrison. The *Saumarez* and four V class destroyers hurried towards her reported position off Sumatra and soon after nightfall H.M.S. *Venus* reported a radar fix at thirty-four miles. The five destroyers advanced in a star-shaped formation, designed to trap the Japanese whichever way they might turn. However, the cruiser turned to face her pursuers in a close-range and confused battle. The *Saumarez* received several 8-inch shell hits but all destroyers launched their torpedoes. No fewer than eight of these are believed to have hit their target, which sank less than fifty miles from Penang. The destroyers then hurried off so as to escape air attacks, which could be expected after daybreak. They reached their base in Ceylon safely, and the Japanese destroyer rescued the survivors of the *Haguro*. That cruiser had been the last but one Japanese heavy unit in South-east Asia. The last, the cruiser *Ashigara*, was sunk three weeks later by the British submarine *Trenchant*.

This should have been, but was not, the last adventure of the *Saumarez*. A year after the war had finished this destroyer and H.M.S. *Volage* fell foul of an undeclared minefield off the Albanian coast. The newly installed communist government of Albania refused to pay any compensation or acknowledge any responsibility for this accident, and it was generally believed that that government took a certain satisfaction in this naval achievement against an ideological enemy. Although the *Volage* was given a new bow, the *Saumarez* never returned to service.

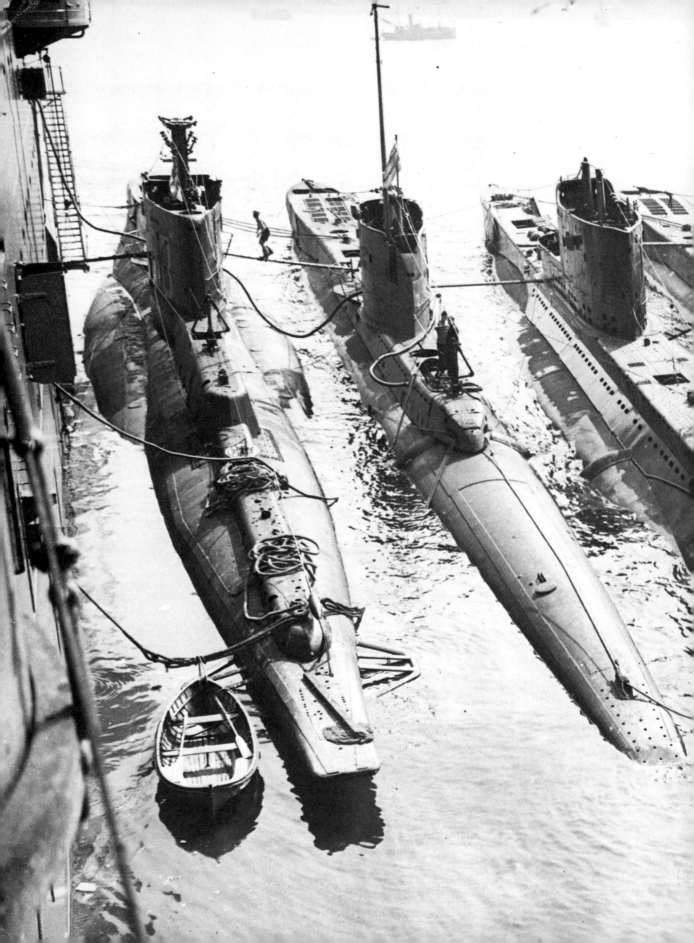

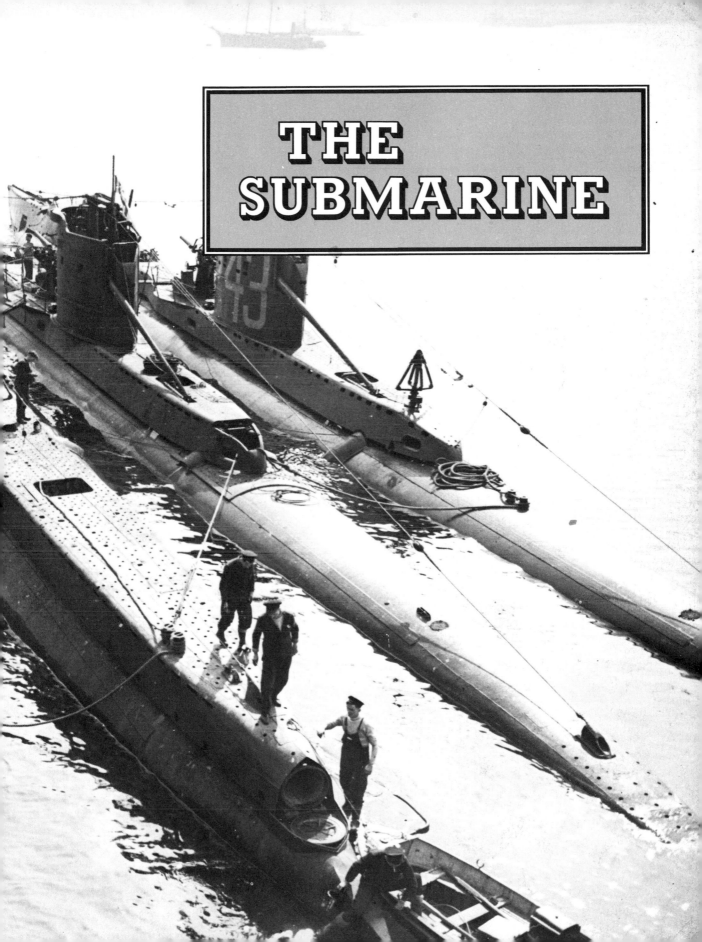

THE SUBMARINE

The submarine first justified itself as a weapon in the First World War. After that war the major navies passed through a period of experimentation intended both to develop the submarine's role and to eliminate its drawbacks. A principal handicap was the submarine's need to carry two sets of motors, diesel for surface propulsion and for battery-charging, and electric for submerged movement. Electric propulsion offered only slow speeds underwater, and required long battery-charging sessions on the surface. But experiments with new types of propulsion were unsuccessful until the closing stages of the Second World War. Several countries built big submarines, loosely termed 'cruiser submarines', which relied on heavy guns rather than torpedoes. Some of these carried a seaplane, intended to seek out targets. The French *Surcouf*, designed for commerce-raiding, carried not only a seaplane but also a motor launch to take boarding parties to intercepted enemy steamers. This submarine also included a compartment designed to accommodate forty prisoners; the French navy ministry, like others, did not anticipate that in the Second World War the submarines of all nations would normally sink enemy freighters without warning and without rescuing survivors.

TYPICAL 'CRUISER SUBMARINES'

	Year of completion	Tonnage on surface	Main guns	Torpedo tubes	Speed (knots): surfaced	submerged
Nautilus, Narwhal (U.S.A.)	1930	2,750	2 6-in	6	17	8
Surcouf (France)	1930	3,000	2 8-in	12	18	10

In the thirties the moderate-sized submarine returned to favour. Most naval powers built small batches of these, trying to evolve the optimum designs. By the end of the decade the U.S.A., Germany and Britain had arrived at designs which were good enough to standardize for large-scale war production. The U.S. Navy had evolved the *Gato* type, a 1,500-ton boat with a long range. Germany was building a series of fifty 250-ton coastal boats but was also constructing so-called 'Atlantic' submarines ranging from 600 to 800 tons, and a larger type of 1,000 tons. Britain, like Germany, had standardized on three basic types. She had the small U class of 550 tons, carrying four or six torpedo tubes and with a range of 4,000 miles. Then there were the intermediate S type (670 tons) and the 1,090-ton T class. France, Japan, Italy and Russia also had considerable submarine fleets. Moreover, since submarines were cheap to build and were capable of opposing the most powerful surface ships, they were also favoured by the smaller navies. Thus during the war both the Allied and Axis navies were reinforced by submarines of the occupied nations.

THE MAIN SUBMARINE POWERS

	Britain	France	Nether-lands	U.S.S.R.	U.S.A.	Germany	Italy	Japan
Total of boats at date of entry into war	57	81	29	250	113	56	122	62
Boats built during war	176	1	0	?	228	1,093	26	118
Boats lost	74	61	18	?	60	785	103	127

N.B. Boats transferred from Britain and the U.S.A. to Allied navies are excluded, as are captured boats and midget submarines.

The above table demonstrates the important role of wartime construction in replacing heavy submarine losses. Despite the rather short expectation of life associated with submarines, none of the belligerents experienced much difficulty in finding crews for the new boats. Wartime construction was on a mass-production basis, concentrated on a few proven designs. The U.S.A. was able to standardize on a single type, while Britain and Germany, needing coastal, medium-range and long-range boats, produced successive modifications of standard designs, although Germany also built numbers of experimental or specialized craft.

The classical submarine tactic, dating from the earliest days, was for a submarine to lie in wait at a chosen location. During the day the horizon would be scanned and the boat would endeavour to get into position to make a submerged attack on whatever target presented itself; if the target was unarmed the submarine might surface and sink it with gunfire. At night the boat would lie on the surface, charging its batteries. These tactics were still used by most navies in the Second World War. However, utilizing their past experience, in the Second World War the Germans favoured attacks by groups of submarines at night on the surface, and

Previous pages: British submarines alongside their depot ship. On the left, with her saddle-tank design clearly shown, is an S-class boat. Next to her is a coastal U-class unit, and in the centre is a T-class boat, with one of her after torpedo tubes clearly visible. Next is H.M.S. *Upright* and finally another U-class boat

Left: Many of the small British U-class submarines were transferred to Allied navies. This is the Royal Netherlands Navy's *Dolfijn*, which in 1943 sank an Italian submarine and several supply ships

believed that submarines should cooperate in seeking targets. These 'wolf pack' tactics were later adopted by the Americans who, however, preferred small groups of about three boats.

During the war, although the Pacific operations of U.S. submarines and the Mediterranean operations of British submarines had great strategic significance, it was the Germans who most fully exploited this weapon. In fact the U-boat campaign, alone among all submarine campaigns, was regarded not as a supporting operation, but as a war-winning operation in its own right. In the First World War submarine attacks on British seaborne trade had at one stage almost won the war for Germany, and German strategists believed that with proper preparation a second U-boat war could be decisive. In this they were probably right, but because Hitler became embroiled in war with Britain several years earlier than expected, the U-boats once again just failed to knock Britain out of the war.

WAR-BUILT SUBMARINES

	Tonnage (surfaced)	Main guns	Torpedo tubes	Speed (knots): surfaced	submerged
Britain					
S type (62 boats)	670	1 3-in	6	14	10
T type (52 boats)	1,100	1 4-in	10	15	9
U and V type (71 boats)	550	1 3-in	4	12	9
U.S.A.					
Gato type (73 boats, Balao type similar)	1,530	1 3-in	10	20	9
Germany					
VIIc type (801 boats)	770	1 3·5-in	5	17	7
IXc type (143 boats)	1,150	1 4·1-in	6	18	7
Japan					
RO-100 type (18 boats)	600	1 3-in	5	14	8
I-15 type (24 boats)	2,200	1 5·5-in	6	23	8

N.B. The I-15 type also carried a seaplane or, later, a midget submarine.

Admiral Dönitz, the First World War submarine officer who commanded the U-boats in the Second World War, had estimated that 300 U-boats were needed to defeat Britain. This number he had planned to build, but when the war started he had only fifty-six. Sixteen of these took up stations in Britain's sea approaches in August 1939, and were in action as soon as war was declared. An early victim was the liner *Athenia*, torpedoed without warning with heavy loss of life. The British were quick to exploit the propaganda value of this 'atrocity', although it seems that the *Athenia* was mistaken by the over-enthusiastic U-boat commander for an armed merchant cruiser. Other early successes were the sinking of one of Britain's few aircraft carriers, the *Courageous*, which the British Admiralty had been unwisely using in anti-submarine operations. U-47 sank the British battleship *Royal Oak*, and

H.M.S. *Sturgeon* drains her conning tower after surfacing

magnetic mines laid by submarines badly damaged the battleship H.M.S. *Nelson* and the cruiser H.M.S. *Belfast*.

However, while the sinking of British warships had great propaganda value, the main task of the U-boats was the destruction of shipping. For success, Dönitz considered it necessary over a sustained period to sink British ships faster than they could be replaced by new construction. This margin of sinkings over new construction was achieved in the early years, but was not maintained for quite long enough. In the first year of the war there were not enough U-boats, and in later years the improvement of anti-submarine defences and the entry into the war of the U.S.A. counterbalanced numerical and technological advances by the Germans.

Prewar U-boat training had emphasized the night attack on the surface, which enabled the submarine to utilize its higher surface speed and manoeuvrability. Only after the attack, and not always then, would the submarine take refuge in the depths. Also, Dönitz had emphasized that submarines would work together. They would be in radio contact with their headquarters, which would enable headquarters, having received a sighting report from one submarine, to direct the others to a rendezvous in the path of the approaching target. The dozen or so submarines thus united would then cooperate in attacking the convoy, making surface attacks at night. During daylight the attacking submarines would withdraw beyond the horizon and then overtake the convoy in readiness for more attacks the following night. One U-boat was enough to shadow a convoy; with its low profile a surfaced submarine could remain unseen by the escorts.

By the end of the first year of war, Dönitz had lost twenty-eight submarines and received twenty-eight new ones. But since new crews had to be trained there were only about thirty operational boats, which meant that on average only seven or eight were at sea at any given time. With such small numbers, 'wolf pack'

Germany began the war with relatively few submarines. U-52 left Kiel in August 1939 to take up station in the Atlantic. In the first year of the war she sank several British freighters

tactics were limited. Nevertheless, combined attacks with a handful of boats sometimes produced spectacular success. In early 1941 a convoy from West Africa to Britain was attacked by a 'wolf pack' consisting of only two submarines, which took turns shadowing the convoy over several days. This convoy consisted of fifty-eight merchantmen, escorted by the battleship *Malaya*, an armed merchant cruiser, and four destroyers. In a series of night surface attacks seven of the freighters were sunk and the *Malaya* damaged. The convoy was then ordered to scatter: evidently the convoy system could be beaten when few escorts were available.

The U-boats would have had even more success if they had been able to locate more convoys. What the submarine service needed was aircraft, but Göring was reluctant to devote precious squadrons to the service of the navy. Thus, despite the unexpected advantage of new advanced bases on the west coast of France, lack of boats and of air reconnaissance prevented Dönitz winning the war for Hitler. Meanwhile the British steadily improved their defences. Air patrols, at first carried out by a few Sunderland flying boats, increased in range and intensity so that submarines on the surface in daylight not only began to suffer casualties but found themselves hindered in their attacks. When aircraft were fitted with radar and searchlights the U-boats were no longer safe on the surface even at night. With air bases established in Northern Ireland, Newfoundland and Iceland, the area of the North Atlantic outside the range of aircraft diminished. Surface escorts also acquired radar and other detection devices, while their numbers increased. British commanders evolved their own anti-submarine tactics, developing the 'killer group' of escorts to counter the 'wolf packs'. The British Admiralty, plotting U-boat positions from German radio activity, learned to divert convoys away from likely submarine concentrations.

In early 1942 U-boat successes reached new heights. The U.S.A. had just entered the war. Off the east coast of America the introduction of a convoy system was long delayed, escorts and aircraft were in the hands of inexperienced crews, and garrulity was such that U-boat commanders could listen in to the local radio stations and not only discover the whereabouts of shipping, but also the routes and schedules of anti-submarine craft. Since few merchantmen were armed, U-boats could safely approach in daylight to attack with gunfire, thus saving expensive torpedoes. (Not only were torpedoes expensive, but U-boats had to return to base when all torpedoes had been expended. This often shortened their cruise and sometimes prevented attacks on sitting targets. In May 1941 H.M.S. *Ark Royal* and H.M.S. *Renown*, hunting the *Bismarck* and unescorted, passed a submerged U-boat at pointblank range, but the submarine had already used its torpedoes.)

As conditions became more difficult in the North Atlantic, submarines were despatched to the South Atlantic and the Indian Ocean. At first these met German ships at prearranged points to take fuel and torpedoes, but after the Royal Navy had rounded up these supply ships large U-boats fitted as tankers replaced the surface supply ships. With Japanese cooperation, some U-boats were stationed at Penang, in Malaya, and these ranged far and wide, reaching Madagascar in the west and Sydney in the southeast. Earlier, to help the Italians, U-boats had been sent to the Mediterranean where, despite losses incurred while passing Gibraltar, they scored successes which included the sinking of the battleship H.M.S. *Barham* and the aircraft carriers H.M.S. *Ark Royal* and H.M.S. *Eagle*.

With British radar usually one step ahead of German countermeasures, with the arrival of U.S. long-range Liberator aircraft, and the proliferation of escort aircraft carriers and of anti-submarine corvettes and frigates, a German victory in the Battle of the Atlantic grew less likely. Dönitz looked to technology as an answer to his problems. Some submarines with hydrogen peroxide propulsion were built, having very fast underwater speeds, and the 'Schnorkel' (or 'snort') was introduced. This was a vertical pipe with an automatic float valve which enabled air to be taken while the submarine was just below the surface. This meant that batteries could be charged without breaking surface: the projecting head of the 'snort' was unlikely to be detected either by eye or radar. Moreover, the device enabled the diesel engines to be used while below the surface, which meant that the submarine had the tactical advantage of a high underwater speed. At the same time some U-boats were built with high capacity batteries which permitted high speeds even below periscope depth, speeds which were often greater than those of the escort ships.

But these and other innovations came too late. Although in early 1945 no fewer than sixty new U-boats were coming into service each month, the results achieved were small. Intense surface and air patrols kept the U-boats away from their targets. Good crews became harder to assemble, despite the rundown of the German surface navy. Of the 40,000 men enrolled in the U-boat service, 28,000 were killed during the war.

The war started badly for the U.S. submarines. Because of the losses and damage suffered at Pearl Harbor, the submarine was virtually the only offensive weapon available. But the speedy loss of bases in the Philippines removed the shorter range submarines from operational availability, while in the first eight months of the war defective torpedoes robbed submarine commanders of several successes. Like the Germans, the Americans placed too much faith in new magnetic torpedoes and in a redesigned contact type, neither of which for financial reasons had been adequately tested. Some torpedoes, additionally, had steering troubles; at least two submarines were sunk by their own torpedoes. Towards the end of the war the Americans, like the Germans, introduced acoustic torpedoes designed to home on the propellers of escort ships.

However, as the war progressed early troubles were overcome and commanders and crews, unlike the Japanese, were quick to learn from experience and to try new tactics. The general strategy of the Pacific war, with troops of both sides moving from island to island, was ideal for submarine activity. The Americans usually succeeded in placing cordons of submarines off islands known to be facing seaborne invasion by one side or other. These submarines then picked off Japanese supply ships and troopships approaching with reinforcements or leaving with fugitives. U.S. submarines were also invaluable as advance scouts. At the Battle of the Philippine Sea, submarines not only warned the U.S. commander of the Japanese movements but also accounted for two of the three Japanese aircraft carriers sunk in that battle. The first action in the Battle for Leyte Gulf was the sinking by submarines of two Japanese heavy cruisers and the reporting by submarines of the Japanese position and course. Earlier, at the Battle of Midway, U.S.S. *Nautilus* had played a key, if accidental, role. This boat, one of the few 'cruiser submarines' to participate in the war, while endeavouring to attack the Japanese was herself depth-charged by a destroyer. It was this destroyer, hurrying back to its force after the unsuccessful attempt to sink the *Nautilus*, which was first spotted by U.S. attack planes. These planes, dive bombers, had been unsuccessfully searching for the Japanese aircraft carriers, but by aligning themselves on the destroyer's course they soon came upon their target and within minutes had changed the course of the war in America's favour.

But although a number of heavy warships and troopships were sunk by U.S. submarines, their main strategic role after the first months was the disruption of supply routes. Japan had started the war largely because she needed oil from the Dutch East Indies, and it was the tankers plying between that territory and Japan which were prime targets. Over a hundred Japanese tankers were sunk, with the result that towards the end of the war neither the Japanese navy nor air force had sufficient fuel to carry out its tasks. The American submarines were aided by the Japanese reluctance to take seriously the convoy system: although convoys were organized they tended to be small and with a single escort. To the

The most successful of the 'cruiser-submarines': U.S.S. *Nautilus* off Alaska in 1943

Japanese martial mind, convoys were 'defensive' and therefore not quite respectable. In 1945 U.S. submarines succeeded in breaking into the Sea of Japan, threatening the routes to China and Manchuria. Hitherto the mines protecting the narrow passages leading into this sea had barred American submarines, but a new sonar device capable of sensing mines enabled a band of gallant submariners to enter the sea and wreak havoc among Japan's diminished merchant navy.

Of all the submarine fleets, that of the Imperial Japanese Navy was provided with the best torpedoes. These were bigger, more reliable – although not infallible – faster, and longer-range than the torpedoes of their enemies. The Japanese submarines were of good design. Some carried midget submarines, but the resources which the Japanese devoted to midget submarines only proved a good investment in one operation. This was carried out by three large submarines off Madagascar. Submarine I-10 launched a seaplane which located the battleship H.M.S. *Ramillies* at Diego Suarez, and submarines I-16 and I-20 launched midgets which badly damaged the battleship and sank a tanker. The midget submarine attack on Sydney a few days later was a fiasco. An old harbour ferry, mistaken for the battleship H.M.S. *Warspite*, was sunk, and a few shells from the confused Allied ships landed ashore, but none of the midgets escaped.

The Japanese submarines started the war without radar, and even when the war ended their radar and sound detection apparatus was of inferior design. More important, with supreme over-confidence the Japanese, ignoring the lessons of the First World War and the advice of German submariners, maintained a strategy which ensured that their submarines would not be used to the best advantage. In the Pacific war their best use would have been against American troop and supply ships, but Japanese naval doctrine laid down that submarines were a fleet weapon, to be deployed against

131

A Japanese submarine is
fished out of Sydney harbour
after the unsuccessful 1942
attack

the enemy's fleet. Thus warships were the prime target, and although there were some successes (like sinking the aircraft carriers U.S.S. *Wasp* and U.S.S. *Yorktown*) this policy was in general unprofitable. There were cases when submarines sank the escort of a convoy and then turned away from the unprotected freighters; to a well-indoctrinated Japanese commander, such ships were unworthy targets. Later in the war Japanese submarines had a new role, carrying supplies to beleaguered island garrisons.

It might be argued that the main contribution of Britain's submarines to the war effort was made by those older boats which acted as targets for anti-submarine training. However, British submarines did at times play an important offensive role. Their most intensive campaign was in the Mediterranean. Interruption of enemy shipping supplying the German and Italian armies in North Africa was essential, and lack of bases and of air superiority meant that submarines were the most suitable instrument for this task. But the narrow, clear, and often shallow waters of the Mediterranean made submarine work hazardous, especially for the larger boats. The small U class units were ideal in this campaign, but even these suffered heavy losses. Of the ninety submarines lost by Britain and the 'free' navies of occupied Europe, fifty-two were sunk in the Mediterranean. However, many Italian vessels were destroyed; apart from all-important troop and supply ships, four Italian cruisers and eleven torpedo craft fell victim to submarine attacks (this excludes an Italian destroyer torpedoed in error by an Italian submarine). Elsewhere, British submarines operated throughout the war off the coast of Norway and, in the East, off Malaya. Some of their successes against warships are mentioned in the Chronology of the War at Sea (see pp. 150). Like the Americans and Germans, the British used an unreliable type of torpedo, but because it was less obviously defective than theirs, its shortcomings passed unheeded until after the end of the war.

The Mediterranean was the most lethal area for British submarines, and the mine the most dangerous weapon. Twenty-six British boats were lost due to mines, and probably a majority of 'cause unknown' losses were also due to them. The following table analyses the cause of British submarine losses in all theatres. It does not include sixteen French, Greek, Polish, Dutch and Norwegian boats lost while operating under British control. Corresponding figures of German losses are given for comparison.

THE SUBMARINE'S ENEMIES

Cause of loss	British submarines lost: units	percentage	German submarines lost: units	percentage
Surface ship	25	34	246	31
Aircraft	6	9	352	45
Combined ship and air attack	—	—	48	6
Submarine	4	5	21	3
Mine	26	35	25	3
Collision	3	4	23	3
Other accidents	—	—	34	5
Friendly forces in error	3	4	?	?
Unknown	7	9	29	4

N.B. German figures exclude U-boats sunk by Russians (probably seven); the 352 units sunk by aircraft include about sixty boats sunk in harbour during the last year of the war. U-boats sunk in error are presumably included under 'other accidents'.

When Italy entered the war in 1940 she had almost twice as many submarines as Germany, and sent forty boats to the Atlantic to help the U-boats. But when the Germans and Italians tried to coordinate their activities there was chaos and ill-will. Finally it was agreed that the Italian submariners would have a patch of the Atlantic for themselves. In this area they had a few scattered successes against shipping, but in general their work was not impressive. They did not lack courage and nerve, but their training and methods were defective. For example, one Italian submarine commander who claimed to have torpedoed a battleship had not only misidentified the target, but had mistaken the explosion of depth charges for the detonation of his torpedoes against the target. In fact the target was not a battleship but a corvette, and his torpedoes had missed.

THE U-47

The U-47 belonged to the VIIb series of boats, one of the 'Atlantic' type. She displaced 753 tons on the surface, although the official declared displacement of this class was 517 tons; this deception enabled Germany to build a greater number of submarines without apparently exceeding the total tonnage limitation stipulated by the Anglo-German Naval Agreement. Launched in 1938 at the Germania Yard, the U-47 was 213 feet long, carried a crew of about thirty-five, and in an emergency could dive to 600 feet. She could crash dive in thirty seconds (fifty seconds from a stationary situation). Surface speed was seventeen knots, and submerged eight knots. With her 108 tons of fuel she could travel 9,500 miles on the surface, while battery capacity was sufficient for a ninety-mile range submerged. She was armed with four bow torpedo tubes and one in the stern and nine reserve torpedoes were stowed. A 3·5-inch gun and a light anti-aircraft gun were also carried.

The U-47 and her commander, Lieutenant Prien, won great fame early in the war by penetrating the British fleet anchorage at Scapa Flow and sinking the battleship *Royal Oak*. German propaganda, which included a 'how I did it' book by Prien, together with British evasion, make it very difficult to reconstruct what actually happened. Contradictions in the German accounts are so evident that some adventurous commentators have denied that the *Royal Oak* was sunk by a submarine at all. But it would seem that as night fell on 13 October 1939 Lieutenant Prien surfaced his boat outside the Scapa Flow approaches. He chose to go through Kirk Sound, which seemed inadequately blocked. There were known to be strong tides in the narrow passages around Scapa, tides which in places ran faster than the speed of the U-boats, but Prien believed that Kirk Sound presented a viable passage (so did the British: an extra blockship had already been earmarked for sinking in this passage). Although there were some difficult moments, Prien managed to take his boat through the

sound and, despite the luminosity shed by the Northern Lights, was unnoticed. Having entered Scapa Flow, he turned northwards towards some warships anchored in the distance. Approaching these, he fired a salvo of four torpedoes. After the expected interval he saw a column of water rise against the side of one of his targets and prepared to make a getaway. But nothing happened; the Flow remained dark and silent. The British had not realized that they had been torpedoed. Somewhat disconcerted, Prien, still on the surface, cruised quietly around the Flow while his crew laboured below to load the reserve torpedoes into the tubes. Reloading finished, the U-47 moved in close for a second attack on the same ship.

Below : Lieutenant Prien is congratulated by Admiral Raeder after sinking the Royal Oak.
Right : U-47: a flag-waving portrait

Another salvo of torpedoes was fired, and H.M.S. *Royal Oak* quickly sank, taking 786 of her crew with her. This time the British did notice that something had happened. Searchlights flashed out, and a destroyer came quite close to the submarine. But the latter, unnoticed, slipped away on the surface. The entire crew received Iron Crosses and Prien was congratulated by Hitler in person.

In 1940, in the Norwegian campaign, the U-47 was patrolling in search of British troopships landing troops in Norway. While she was lying submerged off the Norwegian coast strange metallic noises were heard. These proved to be the anchor chains dropped from a convoy of troopships and its cruiser escort. During the night the U-47 made two attacks, one submerged and one surface. The second was at almost pointblank range on this sitting target, but not a single torpedo exploded on its objective. This disappointing result was found to be the result of defective torpedoes, which, it transpired, had caused many other U-boat commanders to miss their targets. At this time

two detonators were in use, a magnetic detonator which was designed to explode directly underneath the target, and a conventional contact detonator. These were fitted in recently designed torpedoes, but the German torpedo designers had been so enthused by their own genius that they had neglected to carry out proper trials. The result was that the magnetic torpedoes tended to explode before they reached their target, while the contact torpedoes ran too deep, passing beneath. Even when at their proper depth the contact torpedoes often failed to explode.

In early March 1941 a number of U-boats were concentrated for a new intensive attack on convoys in the North Atlantic. Four U-boats, of which Prien's U-47 was one, attacked a westbound convoy over twenty-four hours. Prien took his boat in under cover of a rain squall at dusk, but he was spotted by the old destroyer *Wolverine*. The latter dropped a barrage of depth charges in the area where the submarine had disappeared, and that was the end of the U-47 and Prien.

U.S.S. CAVALLA

U.S.S. *Cavalla* was launched in November 1943 by the Electric Boat Company, the oldest and largest submarine-builder in the U.S.A. She was of the *Gato* class (since 1934, U.S. submarines have been given fish names).

The design of the *Gato* incorporated the experience gained with previous designs, and was chosen for mass production during the war. All war-built submarines were of this type, the *Balao* and *Tench* series being only improvements of the basic design. Intended for Pacific operations, these boats had a long range (12,000 miles) and remarkably good habitability. Displacement was 1,526 tons on the surface and 2,424 tons submerged. Overall length was 312

feet. The designed speed on the surface was just over twenty knots, and nearly nine knots submerged. The oil capacity varied; the *Cavalla* carried 389 tons. There were six torpedo tubes forward, and four more aft. Fourteen spare torpedoes could be stowed. Initially a 3-inch gun was mounted abaft the conning tower, but war experience led to the fitting of an increased anti-aircraft armament; the small gun was replaced by a 5-inch anti-aircraft weapon forward and two 20-mm automatic anti-aircraft guns. Like the Germans, the Americans had decided that the best chance for a submarine attacked by aircraft was to stay on the surface and fight it out, taking advantage of the

submarine's small target area. This class of submarine typically carried a crew of eighty-five men. The safe diving depth was 300 feet, although later units of the *Balao* series were allowed to go down to 400 feet. The design called for an all-welded construction, and this feature facilitated rapid wartime production.

The *Cavalla* distinguished herself at the Battle of the Philippine Sea in 1944. Her report, two days before that battle, of the approach of Japanese forces, enabled the U.S. commander to keep his carriers out of harm's way while U.S. aircraft blunted the Japanese thrust. Not only this, but the *Cavalla* sank the fleet aircraft carrier *Shokaku* in this action. She was able to launch six torpedoes at a range of about 1,000 yards, having moved in with the help of three periscope observations without being spotted by the escorting destroyers. The latter hunted

the submarine for three hours, dropping over a hundred depth charges. Towards the end of those three hours the crew of the submerged *Cavalla* began to hear a different kind of detonation, as bombs stored on the burning *Shokaku* began to explode one by one.

This was the peak of the *Cavalla*'s career – although later in the war she made a night surface attack on the destroyer *Shimotsuki* off Borneo, sinking the ship with two torpedoes. In 1969 she was withdrawn from service but was not scrapped, being sent to Galveston for preservation as a memorial.

U.S.S. Cavalla *as she was towards the end of her career, with modified gun armament*

H.M.S. THUNDERBOLT

During the thirties Britain built several series of submarines of around 1,500 tons. Submarines of this size had a long range (war against Japan was envisaged), but were costly and cumbersome. When it appeared likely that Germany would be Britain's next enemy a smaller patrol submarine was designed. This was the T class, of which fifty-three units were completed between 1939 and 1945. Although outwardly resembling previous types, they were smaller by one-third, displacing about 1,100 tons on the surface. They were 275 feet long and carried from 132 to 230 tons of fuel; six-week patrols were intended and the later boats with 230 tons of oil had a range of 11,000 miles. The complement varied, but was around fifty-five. Ten torpedo tubes were mounted, compared with six in the immediately preceding designs. This was because the Admiralty considered that because of improved anti-sub-

marine detection devices attacks would have to be made at long range, in which circumstances a bigger spread of torpedoes would be needed to achieve a hit. For surface action a 4-inch gun was carried. Maximum speed on the surface was fifteen knots, and nine knots submerged.

The *Thunderbolt* was the third of the type, being completed in 1939. She was originally named *Thetis*, and it was this name which hit the headlines in June 1939. On her acceptance trials, with her crew supplemented by specialists and shipyard workers, she sank in Liverpool Bay. For reasons never satisfactorily explained the bow cap of one of her torpedo tubes had been left open, flooding her two forward compartments. Because rescue operations were unhurried, and because few of the 103 men on board had been properly trained in submarine escape apparatus, only four survived. To many it seemed that the subsequent inquiry, as is

often the case, preferred to attach blame to individuals, rather than question the methods of the Admiralty and the shipbuilders.

After salvage and refit the submarine, re-named *Thunderbolt*, entered service in late 1940. On her first patrol she torpedoed and sank an Italian submarine off the west coast of France. She was then transferred to Halifax, Nova Scotia; because of the shortage of escort ships the Admiralty had decided to use sub-marines as convoy escorts. It was in this role that she was mistakenly shelled by a British merchant cruiser, but without sustaining dam-age. In 1941 the boat was transferred to the Mediterranean, where more submarines were needed to support the North African cam-paign. Here she preyed on enemy shipping, landed special agents in Crete, and transported 'chariots' to Palermo. 'Chariots' were the so-called 'human torpedoes', ridden by two-man crews in diving suits. The *Thunderbolt*'s 'chariots' entered Palermo and sank an Italian cruiser. On her seventh Mediterranean patrol, in 1943, the *Thunderbolt* torpedoed a freighter and was then hunted by the escorting Italian sloop *Cigogna*. The latter's commander was a former submarine officer and was ready to play a waiting game. For one day and two nights the submarine stayed down, skilfully manoeuvring as it heard the 'ping' of the corvette's echo detector striking its hull. But although the submarine prevented the corvette obtaining an accurate fix, by the second morning the oxygen situation must have been desperate. The periscope was raised to see if it was yet possible to surface, but the corvette was close and fired a pattern of twenty-four depth charges. Among the turmoil of explosions the stern of the *Thunderbolt* broke the surface and rose almost vertically before disappearing. Three more depth charges were dropped to make sure, and white chlorine gas began to bubble up to the surface. There were no sur-vivors.

H.M.S. Thunderbolt, *a wartime picture*

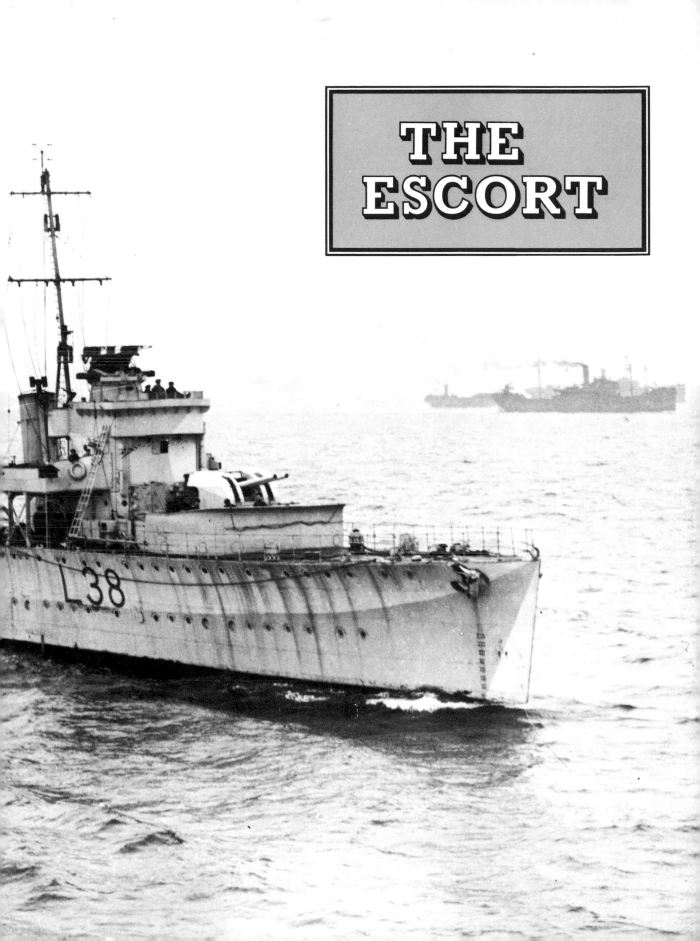

THE ESCORT

he escort is not a type of warship, but rather a collective noun describing a whole group of types. Preoccupation with the bigger and more celebrated ships often obscures the fact that the majority of Second World War warships were small, and were not employed in dramatic battles but in monotonous and perilous protective duties.

In general, the world's navies were poorly prepared to meet submarine and air attack. These threats had not been ignored, but had certainly been underestimated. On the eve of the war the British Admiralty, making good use of the eleventh hour, had ordered the rather novel *Hunt* class destroyers which, unlike existing destroyers, were designed specifically for escort work: speed, torpedo and surface armament were reduced in favour of powerful anti-aircraft and anti-submarine weapons. The *Hunt*s were destined to be among the most successful warship types of the war. Of around 1,000 tons, they carried four or six 4-inch high-angle guns and had a speed of twenty-seven knots. Some carried two or three torpedo tubes, and all were well equipped with anti-submarine weapons. The U.S. 'destroyer escort', of which several hundred were subsequently built, was designed on similar principles.

Apart from the *Hunt*s, Britain had a variety of slower escort ships. There were old destroyers which had been rearmed with 4-inch high-angle guns for escort duties. There were sloops, of which the most distinguished class (the *Black Swan*s) carried six 4-inch high-angle guns and had a speed approaching twenty knots. Soon after the war started, the *Flower* class corvettes began to appear in large numbers. These were small, simple, easy-to-build escorts carrying a 4-inch gun and anti-submarine weapons. The corvettes, many of which were built and manned in Canada, were followed by the frigates, which were bigger but performed the same role. For the defence of coastal convoys the British used trawlers armed with a 4-inch gun. These were slow, but manoeuvrable and seaworthy. Trawlers were not favoured by the U.S.A., which did, however, have a host of submarine-chasers ('PC boats'), armed yachts, and coastguard cutters performing similar duties. Minesweepers were also used as escorts, being equipped with a few guns as well as the paravanes and cutting cables of their main activity. Minesweeping was one of the most essential, monotonous, and dangerous activities of the war, made even harder by the introduction of new types of mine such as the magnetic and acoustic ones.

As the war progressed the depth charge was supplemented by 'Hedgehogs' and 'Squids'. Although a combination of depth charge throwers and depth charge dropping traps could lay a highly destructive and demoralizing pattern of underwater explosions, this pattern had to be laid down when the submarine was too close for observation by ASDIC underwater detection equipment. The new weapons, essentially multi-missile mortars whose bombs exploded on impact, not according to depth, could

Above: One of Britain's
Hunt-class escort destroyers,
H.M.S. *Eglinton*

Previous pages: H.M.S. *Vanity*,
an old destroyer re-equipped
with high-angle guns for
escort duties

throw a pattern of charges well ahead of the attacking ship. At the
same time, increasing numbers of escorts enabled them to work
in groups; this permitted new techniques of attack to be employed.
For example, one ship could keep a submarine under ASDIC
observation while another made the attack.

ASDIC, the echo-sounding underwater detection device, had
been somewhat overrated by the British Admiralty between the
wars. At the time it seemed a remarkable device, but it had drawbacks. It could determine the distance and direction of a submarine, but not its depth (and depth charges had to be set to
explode at the right depth). Moreover, it was 'blind' at close
range, a fact of which German submariners soon took advantage,
knowing that if they remained close to their hunter they could be
undetected. As the war progressed, however, improved forms of
sound detection were devised and fitted. These improvements,
together with radar (which countered the surface tactics with
which the U-boats entered the war), were one key element in the
final victory of escorts over submarines.

The other key element was the escort aircraft carrier. Early in the
war, after long-range German bombers had attacked convoys, the
British as an emergency measure fitted catapults to a few merchant
ships. Each of these catapult-armed ships could launch a solitary
Hurricane fighter which could destroy or drive off the Germans
before ditching near the convoy; the pilot would then wait hope-
fully for a rescue. This was quite a successful innovation, but

Above: PC-611, one of the
U.S. Navy's numerous small
escort vessels

Top right: Canada bore much
of the responsibility for
North Atlantic convoy escorts,
and built several classes of
ship: this is a Canadian
Bangor-class minesweeper

Middle right: The escort
carrier was not designed for
action in the battle-line, but
off Leyte Gulf in 1944 the
U.S. escort carriers were
confronted by Japanese
battleships. Here the U.S.S.
St Lô lays a smoke-screen

Bottom right: At a difficult
stage of the war, to disguise
her lack of battleships, Britain
sent this creation to escort a
Mediterranean convoy. It is
essentially the hull of the old
battleship *Centurion*, with a
wooden superstructure
contrived to resemble a King
George V-class battleship

Above: The *Empire Tide*, one of the British merchant ships fitted with a catapult and Hurricane fighter

clearly wasteful. It was followed by the experimental fitting of a full flight deck to a captured German blockade-runner. This entered service in mid-1941 as Britain's first escort carrier, H.M.S. *Audacity*. She had no elevators, so her six aircraft were stowed on the flight deck, much to the distaste of their mechanics. The *Audacity* was soon sunk by a torpedo, but not before she had demonstrated her value as an anti-submarine weapon. With her aircraft ranging around the convoy, the U-boat packs had difficulty getting into attack positions on the surface. When the aircraft spotted a U-boat, they could summon the surface escorts. In the convoy battle in which the *Audacity* was sunk, only two freighters were lost, but five U-boats were destroyed. In the same year the U.S.A. made her own initial conversion of a merchant ship, resulting in the escort carrier *Long Island* after a rebuild which lasted only three months. During the war the U.S.A. produced eighty-eight escort carriers for herself and another thirty-eight for the Royal Navy, and these cheap and numerous ships, carrying twenty or more aircraft, were invaluable as convoy escorts for the Royal Navy and as providers of air cover for the American amphibious operations. The Japanese also fitted a number of vessels with flight decks, but these were used to replace sunken fleet carriers rather than as escorts.

In general, neither Japan nor Germany were well-provided with escorts when the war started. Japan embarked on a high-priority building programme of ships rather like corvettes, while Germany built numerous minesweepers which could be used as coastal escorts. Both of these countries, feeling the approach of an oil shortage, specified coal-burning boilers for their later escorts.

H.M.S. JERVIS BAY

In both world wars the Royal Navy was short of cruisers and attempted to make up the deficiency by attaching a few guns and White Ensigns to selected liners. The resulting ships were classified as armed merchant cruisers and used mainly as escorts. They were vulnerable ships, being high-sided, unarmoured, and not highly compartmented. In the Second World War they were all disposed of well before the war ended. One of them, the former P. & O. liner *Rawalpindi*, came to a gallant end when confronted by two German battleships, scoring a hit before going down with most of her crew. Another, the former Aberdeen & Commonwealth liner *Jervis Bay*, was destined to become the most celebrated of these unsatisfactory ships.

The *Jervis Bay* was taken over by the Admiralty in August 1939. Seven 6-inch guns, dating from the turn of the century, were distributed around her decks. She was repainted grey and allocated a crew of 255 men (mainly reservists), and the White Ensign was hoisted. Her role was that of ocean escort for Atlantic convoys. In the First World War the Germans had frequently employed armed liners for raiding work, and they did the same in the Second World War. Against such ships the *Jervis Bay* had a good chance of success, but she was no match for armoured ships.

In November 1940 the *Jervis Bay* was the sole escort for a convoy of thirty-seven freighters moving from Halifax to Britain. Earlier, the German 'pocket battleship' *Admiral Scheer* had slipped quietly into the Atlantic. She located the *Jervis Bay*'s convoy and decided to attack immediately, as it was late afternoon and it would be difficult to find targets in the dark. Captain Fegen of the *Jervis Bay* decided to advance to meet the raider, in the hope of delaying the Germans long enough to enable most of the convoy to escape. The convoy was ordered to scatter and the *Jervis Bay*, dropping smoke floats as she went, endeavoured to bring the *Admiral Scheer* within range of her guns.

In this latter aim she never succeeded. Al-

though her guns fired often, every shot fell short of the enemy. Meanwhile 11-inch shells from the raider began to hit. The crew had little protection from blast or from splinters, and casualties were heavy. The bridge was soon hit, and with it the *Jervis Bay*'s gunnery control centre. Captain Fegen lost an arm and soon afterwards was killed by another shell. Most of the officers were killed. Nevertheless, this one-sided battle lasted for twenty-four minutes. At

the end of that period the *Jervis Bay* was ablaze and her guns out of action, and the order was given to abandon ship. Only sixty-five men were picked up, but the sacrifice had not been in vain, for the *Admiral Scheer* only succeeded in destroying five of the freighters in the short time left before nightfall.

During her lifetime H.M.S. Jervis Bay *was virtually unphotographed : this well known picture is from an oil painting commissioned after her celebrated battle*

U.S.S. ENGLAND

Most of the small escort vessels combating submarines and aircraft passed the war in great danger and discomfort with hardly a glimpse of the enemy. Others had perhaps an hour of glory, while a favoured few won fame for the abundance of their victims. In the North Atlantic an escort group consisting of the sloop H.M.S. *Starling* and four sister ships set a record by destroying six U-boats in a cruise of four weeks. This was accomplished by men of great skill and experience, against a well-equipped and competent enemy. But what can be regarded as the all-time record was won by U.S.S. *England*, a newly commissioned ship on her first war operation. She sank six Japanese submarines in twelve days – although in

fairness to the British record it should be said that she was working in calm seas against an enemy who was not very skilful and who did not possess good radar.

The *England* was one of 556 destroyer escorts built by the U.S.A. in its war emergency programmes. The design derived from fifty frigates which the U.S.A. had been building for Britain in 1941. The *England* was of the 24-knot *Buckley* class (1,400 tons, 306 feet long) and carried three 3-inch dual-purpose guns, fourteen light anti-aircraft guns, and three torpedo tubes. Her main anti-submarine weapon was the Hedgehog forward-throwing mortar, but she also had two depth charge racks and other anti-submarine mortars. Her war complement

was 220. She was not named in honour of America's main ally but, like other U.S. destroyers, commemorated a sailor (in this case an ensign killed at Pearl Harbor).

The *England* had only ten weeks of sea experience when she was sent with two other destroyer escorts to hunt Japanese submarines which were being used to supply the garrison at Bougainville. The three ships patrolled in line abreast, listening for a contact. The *England* was the first to make a contact and fired five salvoes from her Hedgehog. Two hits were heard after the second salvo, and three after the fifth. Then there was an underwater explosion so violent that several sailors were thrown flat on the deck and others thought that they had been torpedoed. Oil, debris, and soon a flotilla of circling sharks indicated that the *England* had made her first kill.

Three days later a surfaced submarine was detected by radar seven miles away. By the time the escorts arrived the quarry had submerged. Hedgehog attacks by the *England*'s consorts produced no results, but when the *England* moved in her Hedgehog soon blew up a submarine. The next day there was a similar sequence, with the *England* making a kill after her sisters had failed. On the following day another victim was located on the surface and then destroyed by the *England*'s Hedgehog at a depth of 170 feet. The three ships then turned back to collect more ammunition, but had not progressed far before radar detected yet another submarine eight miles away. Again the first two escorts failed to score hits, but when the *England*'s Hedgehog was brought into play at least four impact explosions were heard at 250 feet. The *England* waited around until daylight to pick up debris to confirm her kill, and went on.

The three ships soon encountered another of their kind, from which they replenished their stock of Hedgehog missiles. All four ships then went to their hunting ground. A contact was made and the commander of the group ordered the *England* to keep clear: he thought that this ship had had enough successes and the others should be given a chance. But the attacks failed, and while the Americans were wondering what to do next the Japanese submarine commander, with more valour than discretion, surfaced and swept the sea with his searchlight. At this the *England* moved in and held the now submerged submarine in her sound detection field, waiting for daylight. At dawn the three other ships made their attack, but once more failed. The *England* was thereupon allowed to try her hand, and a salvo from her Hedgehog elicited an enormous underwater explosion: presumably the Japanese torpedoes had been detonated.

How far the *England*'s success was due to luck and how far to skill is debatable. With sound detection (as with radar) the skill and indeed personality of the operator was a factor whose importance was not fully realized at the time. Similarly, some commanders had a kind of intuitive genius in their timing and placing of Hedgehog salvoes. It is quite possible that the *England* was well-endowed with this kind of asset.

U.S.S. England, *the best known of the U.S. Navy's numerous destroyer-escorts*

CHRONOLOGY OF THE WAR AT SEA

A hero's welcome for the venerable German battleship Schleswig-Holstein, *which began World War II with a bombardment of Polish defences near Danzig*

1939

September   1   Old German battleship *Schleswig-Holstein* begins Second World War by opening fire on Polish coastal defences.

          3   Britain and France declare war. U-30 sinks liner S.S. *Athenia*.

      10   British submarine *Triton* torpedoes British submarine *Oxley* off Norway, the latter thereby becoming both the first British warship to be sunk and the first warship to be sunk by the British in the war.

      14   British submarine *Sturgeon* attacks British submarine *Swordfish*, but her torpedoes miss.

      17   U-29 sinks aircraft carrier H.M.S. *Courageous* off Ireland.

October   14   U-47 sinks battleship H.M.S. *Royal Oak* in Scapa Flow.

| November 23 | German *Scharnhorst* sinks armed merchant cruiser H.M.S. *Rawalpindi*. A magnetic mine, dropped by the Luftwaffe on English mudflats, recovered and examined, enabling counter-measures to be devised. |
| December 13 | Battle of the River Plate, followed by destruction of the German *Graf Spee*. |

1940

February	16	Destroyer H.M.S. *Cossack* disregards Norwegian neutrality to enter fiord, boards German naval supply ship *Altmark*, and rescues British merchant seamen captured earlier by the *Graf Spee*.
	22	German bombers attack two German destroyers in the North Sea; while evading bombs the destroyers run into a minefield and blow up.
April	8	Destroyer H.M.S. *Glowworm* rams German cruiser *Hipper* after being reduced to sinking condition by the latter.
	9	H.M.S. *Renown* encounters German *Scharnhorst* and *Gneisenau* and scores hits. German navy lands troops in Norway, losing cruiser *Blücher* to Norwegian coastal defences.
	10	First Battle of Narvik; two German and two British destroyers sunk. German cruiser *Karlsruhe* irreparably damaged by submarine H.M.S. *Truant* off Norway. Land-based Fleet Air Arm bombers sink German cruiser *Königsberg* at Bergen.
	13	Second Battle of Narvik; eight German destroyers sunk.
	30	Large French destroyer *Maillé Brézé* sinks at Greenock after accidentally discharging a torpedo into her own funnel.
May	10	German invasion of Holland and Belgium.
	26	Troop evacuation from Dunkirk begins, during which six British and seven French destroyers are sunk.
June		A peak month for U-boats, which sink over half a million tons of Allied shipping in June.
	8	Allies end land operations in Norway. Aircraft carrier H.M.S. *Glorious* and two destroyers sunk by German battleships *Scharnhorst* and *Gneisenau*.
	11	Italy declares war against France and Britain.
	25	France signs armistice.
July	3	French warships in British ports seized by Royal Navy. British bombard French squadron at Oran; French retaliate by bombing Gibraltar two days later.
	7	Aircraft carrier H.M.S. *Hermes* and two cruisers damage French battleship *Richelieu* at Dakar.
	9	Encounter off Calabria of British battleships and Italian squadron: one Italian battleship damaged and retiring Italian ships attacked by Italian aircraft in error.
	19	Australian cruiser *Sydney* sinks Italian cruiser *Bartolomeo Colleoni*.
September	5	U.S.A. agrees to transfer to Britain fifty old destroyers and ten escort vessels in exchange for bases in western Atlantic.
	23	Beginning of unsuccessful British and Free French attempt to 'liberate' Dakar from Vichy government.

151

October	10	German *Admiral Scheer* begins cruise against British shipping which will last until April.
	18–20	Seven U-boats sink seventeen out of thirty-four freighters in Atlantic convoy S.C.7 while six U-boats sink fourteen out of forty-nine ships in convoy H.X.79.
November	5	*Admiral Scheer* sinks armed merchant cruiser H.M.S. *Jervis Bay*.
	11	Fleet Air Arm attacks Taranto, sinking Italian battleship *Cavour* and damaging two others.

1941

January	10	German dive bombers badly damage aircraft carrier H.M.S. *Illustrious* in Mediterranean.
	11	German dive bombers sink cruiser H.M.S. *Southampton* in Mediterranean.
February	25	Submarine H.M.S. *Upright* sinks Italian cruiser *Armando Diaz*.
March	28	British and Italian fleets meet off Cape Matapan: Italian heavy cruisers *Pola*, *Gorizia* and *Fiume* and two destroyers sunk by British battleships after Italian withdrawal, which is slowed down by air attacks from carrier H.M.S. *Formidable*.
	31	Italian submarine sinks cruiser H.M.S. *Bonaventure*.
April	24	Royal Navy begins troop evacuation from Greece, losing several destroyers.
May		Long range U-boats appear off West Africa during this month.
	20	Crete operations begin. Cruiser H.M.S. *York*, damaged earlier by Italian motor torpedo boats, is abandoned when Crete is evacuated.
	22	Cruisers H.M.S. *Gloucester* and H.M.S. *Fiji* sunk by German aircraft off Crete.
	24	German *Bismarck* and *Prinz Eugen* sink H.M.S. *Hood* and damage H.M.S. *Prince of Wales* off Iceland.
	27	*Bismarck* destroyed. President Roosevelt commits U.S. forces to protection of Atlantic shipping.
June	3–23	Nine German naval supply ships intercepted in Atlantic and Indian Oceans.
	22	Germany invades Russia.
August	21	First convoy, of seven freighters, leaves for north Russia.
September	4	U.S. destroyer *Greer* attacks U-boats.
October	31	U.S. destroyer *Reuben James*, escorting a convoy, sunk by a U-boat.
November	8	First big success of cruiser Force K: seven German supply ships and one Italian destroyer sunk near Tripoli.
	11	U-81 sinks aircraft carrier H.M.S. *Ark Royal*.
	19	Engagement off Western Australia between cruiser H.M.A.S. *Sydney* and German armed merchant cruiser *Kormoran*; both ships sunk.
	23	U-331 sinks battleship H.M.S. *Barham* and escapes by diving to 820 feet.
December	7	Japanese carrier aircraft put U.S. Pacific Fleet battleships out of action, destroying *Arizona* and *Oklahoma*, but ignore oil storage tanks and repair facilities.

	10	Japanese naval aircraft sink H.M.S. *Prince of Wales* and H.M.S. *Repulse* off Malaya. Japanese land in Philippines. Japanese capture Guam.
	13	Anglo-Dutch destroyer force sinks Italian cruisers *Alberto di Giussano* and *Alberico da Barbiano* off North Africa.
	14	U-557 sinks cruiser H.M.S. *Galatea* near Alexandria.
	17	First Battle of Sirte: British light cruisers pursue two Italian battleships off Benghazi. Beginning of six-day battle between Atlantic Convoy H.G.76 and U-boats: U-boats defeated but escort carrier H.M.S. *Audacity* sunk.
	19	Italian two-man torpedoes severely damage battleships H.M.S. *Queen Elizabeth* and H.M.S. *Valiant* at Alexandria; damage successfully concealed but subsequent damage to H.M.S. *Malaya* leaves Britain without serviceable battleships in Mediterranean. Force K routed in minefield, losing cruiser H.M.S. *Neptune* and sustaining damage to other cruisers.

1942

January	23	Four old U.S. destroyers sink four Japanese transports off Borneo.
	30	Cruiser U.S.S. *Chicago* sunk off Guadalcanal by torpedo planes.
February	12	'Channel dash' of German ships *Scharnhorst, Gneisenau,* and *Prinz Eugen.*
	15	Singapore, Britain's eastern naval base, surrenders to Japanese army.
	19	Japanese carrier aircraft devastate Darwin.
	25	*Gneisenau,* under repair after 'Channel dash', bombed by R.A.F.; never repaired.
	27	Battle of the Java Sea; Dutch cruisers *De Ruyter* and *Java* and two British destroyers sunk by Japanese cruisers.
	28	Cruisers U.S.S. *Houston* and H.M.A.S. *Perth* sink Japanese transports before being overwhelmed by cruisers.
March		Half a million tons of Allied shipping sunk in this month, mostly by U-boats sent to American waters.
	1	Cruiser H.M.S. *Exeter* and two destroyers sunk by Japanese cruisers near Java.
	11	U-565 sinks cruiser H.M.S. *Naiad* in Mediterranean.
	22	Second Battle of Sirte; British light cruisers and destroyers using smokescreens and torpedoes drive off Italian battleship and cruisers attacking Malta convoy, but German aircraft destroy almost all cargoes.
	27	British naval and commando raid on St Nazaire puts out of action only dry dock on Atlantic suitable for German battleship *Tirpitz.*
April		In this month Japan begins to use convoy system.
	1	Italian cruiser *Delle Bande Nere* sunk by submarine, H.M.S. *Urge.*
	5	Japanese carrier aircraft raid Colombo, and also sink cruisers H.M.S. *Dorsetshire* and H.M.S. *Cornwall.*

	9	Japanese carrier aircraft raid Trincomalee, and also sink aircraft carrier H.M.S. *Hermes*. Japanese cruisers operate against shipping in Bay of Bengal.
	18	U.S. carrier aircraft bomb Tokyo.
	20	Aircraft carrier U.S.S. *Wasp* makes first of two deliveries of new R.A.F. fighters to Malta, where German air bombardment has intensified.
May	2	Cruiser H.M.S. *Edinburgh* sunk by German destroyers in Barents Sea.
	4–8	Battle of the Coral Sea; carriers U.S.S. *Lexington* and smaller Japanese *Shoho* sunk, and Japanese landing at Port Moresby frustrated.
	5	To prevent possible use by enemy, Madagascar invaded by British and Free French with strong naval support; three Vichy French submarines sunk while opposing landings.
	15	Cruiser H.M.S. *Trinidad*, after torpedoing herself with errant torpedo, is sunk by German aircraft in Barents Sea.
	29	Japanese midget submarine badly damages battleship H.M.S. *Ramillies* off Madagascar.
	31	Japanese midget submarines fail at Sydney.
June		This is a peak month for U-boats, over 800,000 tons of Allied shipping being sunk.
	3–5	Battle of Midway: timely intelligence and good fortune enable U.S. ships to avoid submarine and carrier trap and then destroy Japanese carriers *Akagi*, *Kaga*, *Soryu* and *Hiryu*, the cruiser *Mikuma*, and 322 planes for the loss of carrier U.S.S. *Yorktown*, a destroyer, and 150 planes, thereby changing the course of the war in America's favour.

During the Dakar fiasco in 1940: the F-class destroyer H.M.S.
Foresight lowers a boat to take de Gaulle to a conference on H.M.S.
Barham *(in background)*

	11	Two convoys sent to Malta but only two freighters arrive; in these operations Italian cruiser *Trento* and British cruiser *Hermione* are sunk by submarines.
	27	Convoy P.Q.17 leaves for north Russia but only thirteen of its thirty-three merchant vessels arrive; convoys to Russia suspended until September.
July		Air attacks on beleaguered Malta decline in this month, and first British submarines return to their base there.
August	7	U.S. marines land on Guadalcanal, the first step in pushing back the Japanese.
	8	Battle of Savo Island: Japanese cruisers achieve surprise in night attack and sink cruisers U.S.S. *Quincy*, U.S.S. *Vincennes*, U.S.S. *Astoria* and H.M.A.S. *Canberra*.
	9	U.S. submarine S-44 sinks Japanese cruiser *Kako* off Rabaul.
	11	Aircraft carrier H.M.S. *Eagle*, on convoy duty in Mediterranean, sunk by U-73.
	13	Cruiser H.M.S. *Manchester* sunk by Italian motor torpedo boats.
	24–5	Battle of Eastern Solomons; aircraft from U.S.S. *Saratoga* sink Japanese carrier *Ryujo* but U.S.S. *Enterprise* damaged; Japanese abandon operation to reinforce their Guadalcanal troops.
September	15	Japanese submarine sinks U.S.S. *Wasp* and damages battleship U.S.S. *North Carolina*, leaving U.S.A. with one operational carrier and one operational new battleship in Pacific.
October	11	Battle of Cape Esperance; U.S. cruisers in a confused night action sink a Japanese cruiser and destroyer and also an American destroyer.
	26	Battle of Santa Cruz Islands; Japanese carrier aircraft sink U.S.S. *Hornet*, and U.S.S. *Enterprise* saved only by anti-aircraft gunfire from battleship U.S.S. *South Dakota*, but Japanese lose 100 aircraft against U.S. loss of seventy-four.
November	8	Allied troops conveyed safely to Morocco and Algeria; three French destroyers and eight submarines sunk while resisting the landings and French battleship *Jean Bart* damaged in gun duel with U.S.S. *Massachusetts*.
	12–15	Confused battles off Guadalcanal result in sinking of Japanese battleships *Hiei* and *Kirishima* and of U.S. cruisers *Atlanta* and *Juneau*, while air attacks sink a Japanese cruiser; this is the last attempt by Japanese to relieve Guadalcanal with major warships.
	15	Escort carrier H.M.S. *Avenger* sunk by U-155 in Atlantic.
	30	Battle of Tassafaronga: unsuccessful U.S. night operation in which cruiser U.S.S. *Northampton* sunk and three other cruisers badly damaged by Japanese destroyers' torpedoes.
December	4	Italian cruiser *Attendolo* sunk by air attack at Naples.
	31	German heavy ships repelled by destroyer escort of Russian convoy. Admiral Raeder decides to resign his command of German navy and is soon replaced by Dönitz.

1943

January 3 Italian cruiser *Ulpio Traiano* sunk by British 'human torpedo' while being completed at Palermo.

March 2 Battle of the Bismarck Sea, in which U.S. land-based aircraft sink eight transports and four destroyers of a Japanese convoy attempting to reinforce New Guinea troops; future reinforcements will be sent by submarine or barge.

26 Indecisive cruiser action off Komandorski Islands in the Aleutians.

April 10 Italian cruiser *Trieste* sunk by air attack.

28 Beginning of eight-day convoy battle, marking turning point of Battle of the Atlantic; fifty-one U-boats confront Convoy O.N.S.5 but seven escorts with air assistance sink six submarines and drive off others for the loss of twelve freighters.

May In this month, thanks largely to superior Allied radar, forty-one U-boats are destroyed.

July In this month, for the first time, Allied merchant ship construction exceeds losses.

6 Battle of Kula Gulf, a night cruiser action in which U.S.S. *Helena* is sunk by a torpedo.

9 Troops conveyed safely to Sicily and Allied ships give gunfire support to landings.

13 Battle of Kolombangara, a night cruiser battle in which a Japanese light cruiser and U.S. destroyer are sunk.

August 6 Battle of Vella Gulf, a night destroyer action in which U.S. ships sink three Japanese destroyers.

September In this month British Eastern Fleet transfers its base from Kenya to Ceylon.

8 Italian armistice signed.

9 Salerno landings begin; cruisers H.M.S. *Uganda* and U.S.S. *Savannah* badly damaged by glider bombs. Most of Italian fleet surrenders to Allies but battleship *Roma*, en route to Malta, is blown up by German glider bomb.

19 British midget submarines damage German battleship *Tirpitz* in Norwegian fiord.

October 6 Battle of Vella Lavella, a night action in which both U.S.A. and Japan lose a destroyer, but the Japanese succeed in evacuating their troops from the island.

23 Cruiser H.M.S. *Charybdis* sunk by German destroyers off French coast.

November 2 Battle of Empress Augusta Bay, another confused night battle in the Solomons, in which both sides suffer collisions and fire on their own ships; a Japanese light cruiser sunk.

25 Battle of Cape St George, a night destroyer action in the Solomons in which two Japanese destroyers sunk by U.S. torpedoes.

December 26 German battleship *Scharnhorst* sunk at Battle of North Cape.

28 Cruisers H.M.S. *Glasgow* and H.M.S. *Enterprise* sink three German destroyers in Bay of Biscay.

1944

January	29	Cruiser H.M.S. *Spartan* sunk by German aircraft off Anzio.
February	17	U.S. carriers, battleships and submarines attack Truk, the 'Gibraltar of Japan', sinking two cruisers.
	18	Cruiser H.M.S. *Penelope* sunk by U-410 in Mediterranean.
March	30	British carrier aircraft damage German battleship *Tirpitz*.
April		In this month U-boat campaign in Atlantic is suspended, pending delivery of improved types of submarine.
June	6	D-Day; troops safely conveyed to Normandy, while naval gunfire support begins.
	19–21	Battle of the Philippine Sea, in which Japanese fail to win anticipated great naval victory and lose carriers *Taiho* and *Shokaku* to U.S. submarines and *Hiyo* to carrier aircraft.
August		In this month U-boats are transferred from threatened French ports to Norway.
	15	Invasion of southern France.
September		In this month U-boats begin campaign in British coastal waters.
October 10 15		U.S. carrier planes attack Okinawa, Luzon, and Formosa and Japanese claim to sink eleven carriers, two battleships and three cruisers in their counterattacks; big victory celebrations in Tokyo but actual U.S. losses are only eighty-nine aircraft.
	23	First phase of Leyte Gulf battles; U.S. submarines sink advancing Japanese cruisers *Atago* and *Maya*.
	24	In Sibuayan Sea Kurita's force, virtually without air cover, is attacked by carrier planes and loses battleship *Musashi*, but Japanese land-based planes sink carrier U.S.S. *Princeton* while Admiral Halsey's ships move north to attack Japanese 'bait' carriers and thereby uncover Leyte Gulf.
	25	Climax of Battle for Leyte Gulf; Japanese battleships *Yamashiro* and *Fuso* destroyed in Surigao Strait and remainder of this Southern Force retires but subsequently loses damaged cruiser *Mogami*; Halsey's aircraft sink Japanese carrier *Chitose* and damage carriers *Zuiho*, *Zuikaku* and *Chiyoda*, which are finished off later while Halsey takes his ships back south, while off Samar Kurita's Centre Force sinks U.S. escort carrier *Gambier Bay* but loses cruisers *Chokai*, *Chikuma* and *Suzuya* to destroyer and air attacks before retiring. Including the U.S. escort carrier *St Lô*, sunk by suicide planes, U.S. losses in these battles are one fleet carrier, two escort carriers, and three destroyers, against Japanese losses of three battleships, four carriers, nine cruisers, and nine destroyers (this including four light cruisers sunk by air attack in the Philippines).
November	12	British bombers sink German battleship *Tirpitz* in Norwegian fiord.
	21	U.S. submarine *Sealion* sinks Japanese battleship *Kongo*.
	28	U.S. submarine *Archerfish* sinks new Japanese aircraft carrier *Shinano*.
December	17	U.S. Navy loses three destroyers and 186 planes in typhoon.

1945

January	4	U.S. escort carrier *Ommaney Bay* sunk by suicide plane off Philippines.
February	19	Iwo Jima landings begin; suicide planes sink escort carrier U.S.S. *Bismarck Sea* and badly damage U.S.S. *Saratoga* in these operations.
March	18–19	Carrier planes bomb airfields in southern Japan.
	30	U.S. aircraft sink German cruiser *Köln* at Wilhelmshaven.
April	1	Okinawa landings begin.
	6	'Last sortie' of Japanese navy; battleship *Yamato* and cruiser *Yahagi* with two destroyers sunk by carrier aircraft en route to Okinawa.
	9	German *Admiral Scheer*, *Emden*, and *Hipper* irreparably damaged by R.A.F. bombing at Kiel.
	16	German battleship *Lützow* damaged by R.A.F., and never repaired.
May	4	U-boats ordered to cease hostilities.
	7	Dönitz, former U-boat officer and Hitler's successor, authorizes Germany's surrender.
	12	Forty-second and final eastbound convoy sails for Russia.
	16	British destroyers sink Japanese cruiser *Haguro* near Penang.
June	8	British submarine *Trenchant* sinks Japanese cruiser *Ashigara* off Sumatra.
	21	Americans complete capture of Okinawa.
July	17	U.S. carriers and battleships, with British contingent, begin raids on Yokosuka, Kure, and Japanese airfields.
	30	U.S. cruiser *Indianapolis* sunk by Japanese submarine. British midget submarines irreparably damage Japanese cruiser *Takao* at Singapore.
September	2	Japanese surrender signed on board battleship U.S.S. *Missouri* in Tokyo Bay.

A photograph printed by countless newspapers in 1942: the Japanese cruiser Mikuma *sinking after the Battle of Midway*

Acasta, 34
Achilles, 32, 90, 102, 104
Admiral Scheer, 15, 16, 19, 21, 29, 30, 31, 146-7, 152, 158
Ajax, 32, 90, 102-04
Akagi, 58, 61, 65, 71, 78-9, 154
Alabama, 18, 23, 42-4
Alaska, 14, 18
Alberico da Barbiano, 92, 117, 153
Alberto di Giussano, 92, 153
Andrea Doria, 19
Anson, 17, 40
Archerfish, 157
Arethusa, 87, 90, 94, 102
Argonaut, 89, 91
Argus, 58, 61
Arizona, 15, 18, 50, 152
Ark Royal, 10, 38, 60, 61, 66-8, 129, 152
Arkansas, 18, 51
Ashigara, 92, 121, 158
Astoria, 91, 155
Atago, 47, 92, 157
Atlanta, 95, 155
Audacity, 145, 153
Avenger, 155

Baltimore, 91, 93, 100
Barham, 6-7, 15, 17, 48, 129, 152, 154
Bartolomeo Colleoni, 85, 92, 151
Béarn, 61
Belfast, 88, 91, 105-07, 127
Bismarck, 13, 14, 15, 19, 36-9, 41, 42, 50, 67, 68, 108, 129, 152
Blücher, 108, 109, 151
Boise, 91, 100-01
Bonaventure, 91, 152
Bretagne, 15, 17
Brooklyn, 88, 91, 98, 100

Caio Duillio, 19
Calabria, action off, 48
California, 18, 50
Canberra, 90, 155
Cape Esperance, battle of, 46, 94, 100, 155
Cape Matapan, battle of, 49, 63, 103, 152
Cape Spartivento, battle of, 67
Cavalla, 136-7
Centurion, 144
"Channel Dash", 34, 108-09, 153
Charybdis, 91, 117, 156
Chicago, 91, 153
Chikuma, 92, 157
Chitose, 92, 157
Chiyoda, 92, 157
Chokai, 92, 157
Cleveland, 91, 93, 100
Colorado, 18

Conti di Cavour, 15, 19, 152
Coral Sea, battle of, 64, 71-2, 73, 77, 80, 154
Cornwall, 78, 90, 153
Cossack, 151
Courageous, 58, 59, 61, 62, 66, 126, 150
Courbet, 17
Cumberland, 32, 89, 90

Dido, 88, 89, 91, 93, 103
Dorsetshire, 78, 90, 153
Duke of York, 2, 17, 34, 40-1, 107, 120
Dunkerque, 14, 17, 28, 38

Eagle, 58, 61, 129, 155
Eastern Solomons, battle of, 155
Edinburgh, 88-9, 91, 105, 106, 154
Eglinton, 143
Emden, 91, 158
Empire Tide, 145
England, 148-9
Enterprise (H.M.S.), 90, 156
Enterprise (U.S.S.), 45, 46, 61, 64, 69-73, 74, 75, 76, 79, 80, 99, 155
Essex class, 62, 65, 69
Exeter, 86, 90, 94, 102, 153

Fiji, 91, 152
Fiume, 92, 152
Foresight, 154
Formidable, 61, 152
Furious, 58, 61
Furutaka, 85, 92, 101
Fuso, 15, 19, 23, 99, 157

Galatea, 90, 153
Gambier Bay, 55, 157
Giulio Cesare, 19
Glasgow, 90, 156
Glorious, 16, 34, 58, 61, 63, 66, 151
Gloucester, 90, 152
Glowworm, 151
Gneisenau, 13, 15, 19, 33, 34, 36, 67, 108, 151, 153
Gorizia, 92, 152
Graf Spee, 14, 15, 19, 28-32, 93, 102, 151
Grayling, 99
Greer, 152
Guadalcanal, battle of, 22-3, 46, 55, 72, 94, 95, 155
Guam, 18

Haguro, 92, 121, 158
Haruna, 15, 19, 53, 54, 55
Heerman, 113
Helena, 91, 156
Hermes, 54, 58, 59, 61, 78, 151, 154
Hermione, 91, 155

Hiei, 15, 19, 53, 55, 72, 95, 155
Hipper, 92, 108, 109, 117, 151, 158
Hiryu, 61, 65, 72, 80, 154
Hiyo, 62, 157
Hood, 15, 17, 37, 108, 152
Hornet, 46, 61, 64, 69, 71, 74-5, 155
Hosho, 58, 61
Houston, 91, 98, 153
Howe, 17, 40
Hyuga, 15, 19

Idaho, 18
Illustrious, 60, 61, 62, 63, 152
Implacable, 61
Indefatigable, 61
Independence, 62, 73
Indiana, 18, 42
Indianapolis, 91, 96-7, 158
Indomitable, 61
Iowa, 14, 18, 23, 29
Ise, 19
Italia, 19

Java Sea, battle of, 94, 98, 153
Jean Bart, 17, 155
Jervis Bay, 146-7, 152
Johnston, 116, 118-9
Juneau, 95, 155
Junyo, 62

Kaga, 58, 61, 71, 78, 154
Kako, 85, 92, 155
Karlsruhe, 91, 151
Kenya, 89, 90
King George V, 13, 14, 15, 17, 25, 29, 38, 40, 41, 42, 54
Kinugasa, 72, 92
Kirishima, 15, 19, 23, 46, 47, 53, 55, 155
Köln, 91, 158
Kongo, 15, 19, 29, 52-5, 118
Königsberg, 63, 91, 151
Kumano, 92, 118

Leander, 87, 90, 94, 102, 103
Leipzig, 91, 109
Lexington, 56-7, 59, 61, 64, 69, 76-7, 154
Leyte Gulf, battle of, 23, 26-7, 44, 47, 55, 65, 72, 81, 99, 101, 113, 117, 118-9, 130, 144, 157
Long Island, 145
Lorraine, 17
Lützow, 15, 19, 28, 29, 30, 31, 117, 158

Malaya, 17, 44, 48, 128, 153
Manchester, 90, 117, 155
Marat, 15, 19
Maryland, 18

Massachusetts, 18, 23, 42, 155
Maya, 92, 157
Midway, battle of, 55, 64, 65, 79, 80, 98-9, 130, 154
Mikuma, 72, 92, 98, 99, 154, 158
Mississippi, 18
Missouri, 18, 158
Mogami, 88, 92, 98-9, 100, 105, 157
Musashi, 15, 19, 24, 26, 157
Mutsu, 15, 19
Myoko, 85, 86, 92

Nachi, 92, 99
Nagato, 19, 21, 53
Naiad, 91, 153
Narvik, battle of, 48, 116, 151
Nautilus, 130, 131
Nelson, 9, 10, 17, 127
Neptune, 90, 94, 103, 153
Nevada, 18
New Jersey, 18, 44
New Mexico, 18
New Orleans, 87, 91
New York, 18, 50, 51
Norfolk, 37, 90, 107
North Cape, battle of, 34, 40
North Carolina, 18, 23, 42, 45-6, 47, 155
Northampton, 91, 155

Okinawa, operations, 51, 73, 96
Oklahoma, 15, 18, 152
Oktyabrskaya Revolyutsia, 18
Onslow, 117
Orion, 90, 103

Paris, 17
Parizhskaya Kommuna, 18
Pearl Harbor, attack, 64, 65, 69-71, 76, 78, 80, 87, 130, 149
Penelope, 90, 102, 157
Pennsylvania, 18, 50
Pensacola, 86, 87, 91
Perth, 90, 98, 153
Philippine Sea, battle of, 65, 72, 81, 130, 137, 157
Phoenix, 91, 101
Pola, 92, 152
Portland, 70, 91, 96
Prince of Wales, 15, 17, 37, 38, 40, 41, 54, 108, 152, 153
Princeton, 157
Prinz Eugen, 34, 36, 92, 108-09, 152, 153
Provence, 17

Queen Elizabeth, 10, 17, 48, 153
Quincy, 91, 155

Ramillies, 17, 131, 154
Ranger, 59, 61
Rawalpindi, 34, 146, 151
Regolo, 88, 92
Renown, 10, 17, 32, 34, 67, 68, 129, 151
Repulse, 10, 11, 15, 17, 54, 153
Resolution, 10, 17, 66
Reuben James, 152
Revenge, 17
Richard Beitzen, 113
Richelieu, 13, 17, 22, 66, 151
River Plate, battle of, 29, 32, 86, 102, 103, 104, 151
Rodney, 9, 10, 17, 88
Roma, 15, 19, 156
Royal Oak, 15, 17, 126, 134, 135, 150
Royal Sovereign, 17, 21
Ryujo, 61, 155

Salt Lake City, 86, 87, 91, 101
San Diego, 88, 91
San Francisco, 91, 100
Santa Cruz, battle of, 46, 72, 75, 155
Saratoga, 56–7, 59, 61, 69, 72, 76, 155, 158
Saumarez, 120–1
Savage, 120–1
Savannah, 91, 101, 156

Savo Island, battle of, 94–5, 100, 155
Scharnhorst, 13, 14, 15, 16, 19, 20, 33–5, 36, 40, 41, 45, 63, 67, 107, 108, 120, 151, 153, 156
Schleswig-Holstein, 15, 19, 28, 150
Schliesen, 15, 19, 28
Scorpion, 120
Sealion, 55, 157
Shaw, 110
Sheffield, 67, 91, 107
Shimotsuki, 137
Shinano, 26, 62, 157
Shoho, 62, 64, 77, 154
Shokaku, 61, 64, 65, 72, 75, 77, 80, 81, 137, 157
Sirte, battle of, 93
Soryu, 61, 65, 71, 154
South Dakota, 14, 18, 23, 42, 46, 47, 75, 155
Southampton, 88, 90, 105, 152
Spartan, 91, 157
St Lô, 144, 157
Stord, 120
Strasbourg, 15, 17, 21, 66
Sturgeon, 127, 150
Suffolk, 37, 90
Surcouf, 125
Suzuya, 92, 157
Swordfish, 150

Sydney, 85, 90, 94, 102–3, 151, 152

Taiho, 55, 62, 157
Takao, 47, 85, 92, 158
Tambor, 98
Taranto attack, 63, 64, 152
Tassafaronga, battle of, 95, 155
Tennessee, 18
Texas, 18, 23, 50–1
Thunderbolt, 138
Tirpitz, 15, 19, 20, 36, 38, 40, 153, 156, 157
Trenchant, 121, 158
Trento, 85, 92, 155
Tribal class, 112, 114, 115, 117
Trident, 109
Trieste, 85, 92, 156
Trinidad, 91, 154
Truant, 151

U-29, 150
U-47, 134–5, 150
U-52, 128
U-73, 155
U-81, 152
U-331, 152
Uganda, 91, 156
Upright, 122, 152
Urge, 153

Valiant, 10, 17, 48, 153
Vanity, 140
Vella Gulf, battle of, 116, 156
Vella Lavella, battle of, 156
Venus, 121
Victorious, 38, 47, 61, 72
Vincennes, 91, 155
Vittorio Veneto, 13, 19

Warspite, 10, 17, 45, 48–9, 50, 131
Washington, 2, 14, 18, 23, 25, 33, 42, 45–7, 54
Wasp, 45, 61, 69, 75, 132, 154, 155
West Virginia, 18
Wichita, 88, 91, 93, 100
Wisconsin, 18
Worcester, 109

Yahagi, 92, 119, 158
Yamashiro, 15, 19, 23, 99, 101, 157
Yamato, 14, 15, 19, 24–7, 28, 53, 118, 158
York, 86, 90, 152
Yorktown, 61, 64, 65, 69, 71–2, 73, 74, 77, 132, 154

Zuiho, 62, 157
Zuikaku, 61, 72, 80–1, 157

Index compiled by J. van den Broeke